SHIFT

12 Keys to Shift Your Life

by

Tracy Latz, M.D., M.S.
Marion Ross, Ph.D., Mh.D.

authorHOUSE®

AuthorHouse™
1663 Liberty Drive, Suite 200
Bloomington, IN 47403
www.authorhouse.com
Phone: 1-800-839-8640

First published by AuthorHouse   2/15/2008

ISBN: 978-1-4343-6281-0 (sc)
ISBN: 978-1-4343-6282-7 (hc)

Library of Congress Control Number: 2008900324

Printed in the United States of America
Bloomington, Indiana

This book is printed on acid-free paper.

Additional Materials Are Available

There is a set of companion CDs containing all
of the meditations presented in the 12 Keys.
For more information about how to
purchase them, go to our website:
www.12keystoshift.com

Acknowledgements

Our deep appreciation goes to our wonderful teachers who encouraged us from kindergarten through graduate school and Delphi University, as well as to Fabien Maman, Bill O'Hanlon, and all of our students who inspired us. We also wish to thank Mark Lighton for his talented editing and helpful comments and Nani for her talent in creating four of our excellent illustrations (joyful cartoons are the work of Tracy).

From Tracy: I would like to express my sincere gratitude to my three incredible, beautiful children (Erin, Nicholas and Austin) who are bright Lights in my life and have been so supportive and understanding of the hours their mother spent working on this manuscript. Thanks to my own talented mother (Pat Thompson) for her constant love and support in all my endeavors and her sage advice, my sisters Allison and Cheryl for their Baba Yaga Sisterhood (you know how I feel), my brother Mark and his wife Sandy for their support (more than words can say), and my brother Brad whose presence I can feel from a continent away. Dad, thanks for the lessons you taught me that I didn't understand until you were gone from this physical realm.

From Marion: Many thanks to my mother, dear friends and godchildren on several continents for all of their love and support. I would like to give a special thanks to Andre for his enthusiasm, support and assistance, technical and otherwise. Much gratitude and appreciation goes to Billie Ross and my dad Howard for being test subjects for our techniques and tools and for all their love and encouragement throughout this project.

Contents

SHIFT: 12 Keys to Shift Your Life

Stuck = caught or held in a position from which it is impossible to move; not able to find a solution or way out of a situation

Introduction

Are you feeling stuck? In your circumstance? In your relationship? In your physical condition? In your life? Would you like to remove the obstacles in your path that prevent a more joyful flow in your life? Are you frustrated with an inability to put well-meaning concepts described in popular books and film to positive benefit in your life?

This book is for anyone, like us, who has ever felt blocked in their ability to move forward, an inner restlessness, an emptiness, or a sense that there must be more to life than their experience up until this moment. Essentially, this book is for anyone who is interested in overcoming the hurdles which keep us stuck or prevent us from moving forward. The 12 Keys will give you the resources to understand why you are stuck and explain how you can make different choices to begin moving in your life.

Why is this book different? This is a how-to book for those of you interested in learning a combination of proven age-old techniques and modern energy psychology practices and applying it to disperse the obstacles blocking your path. These techniques are for you to add to the current tools you may already be using, whether those are medication, individual psychotherapy, nutritional or ayurvedic approaches. We do not encourage you to either stop or adjust medication without consulting your treating physician or healthcare practitioner.

We don't give empty promises. Rather we offer you the option to choose to begin your own journey unencumbered. If you use the techniques we describe in each of our 12 Keys, you will see positive transformation in your life. It may not happen overnight; the journey for each is a personal one. Some may see shifts in their experiences sooner than others as everyone moves at their own speed.

We give specific practical tools and short exercises to remove self-sabotaging roadblocks in order to create shifts in your life. We offer "the toolbox" to become centered and assist you in removing whatever obstacle is preventing you from experiencing abundance today. You may use this book from start to finish as an intensive personal healing journey during which you shift your situation or jump start your life; or you may use it as a reference guide to be consulted a chapter at a time whenever a specific issue or challenge arises and stalls forward momentum in your life.

Each of the 12 Keys presented in our book addresses a specific obstacle:

Key 1. The Obstacle of Feeling Unloved
Key 2. The Obstacle of Guilt and Shame
Key 3. The Obstacle of Abandonment
Key 4. The Obstacle of Anger and Resentment
Key 5. The Obstacle of How We Define Our Self
Key 6. The Obstacle of Lack of Self-Love
Key 7. The Obstacle of Inadequacy and Powerlessness
Key 8. The Obstacle of Heartache
Key 9. The Obstacle of the Unknown
Key 10. The Obstacle of Stress
Key 11. The Obstacle of Habit
Key 12. The Obstacle of Self-Discipline

Each Key will include at least one exercise and meditation for removing the obstacle being addressed and real-life examples of people who have used these techniques to shift their lives into gear.

About the Authors

So how exactly did an international business entrepreneur and a physician (a psychiatrist no less) get together to write a book on the 12 Keys?

For the first 50 years of Marion's life, she had been too busy focusing on what she deemed to be success to reflect upon her health or the possibility that she was stuck. An ache was just another distraction, something a pill or supplement could fix. Her interests were limited to: success in her business career, consulting for major corporations, getting her golf handicap under 6, traveling, and creating a multitude of international projects. Being a hyperactive, overachieving, type A personality, Marion had repeatedly ignored the many physical hints to consider change. Since her teenage years, she had suffered from knee problems, back pain and biannual bouts with bronchitis and tonsillitis. One morning the message from the universe grew louder. Her shoulder completely froze and she couldn't put her coat on. It was 12 degrees outside.

Orthopedists couldn't help, physical therapy was useless and modern drugs failed her. After searching for six months for a traditional allopathic cure, she still couldn't raise her arm. Marion spent countless sleepless nights tossing and turning due to pain. The day finally dawned when she felt compelled to seek other options.

The very morning that she decided to find out what other treatment options were available Marion ran into an old friend in Paris. Although she hadn't seen this friend in ages, he was very worried when she winced with pain as she tried to hug him in greeting. He mentioned that he had recently changed careers transitioning from investment banking to holistic healing.

He offered to take Marion home with him, put her on his massage table and facilitate the healing of her aching shoulder. That was a peculiar statement coming from the Philippe whom she had known for over 30 years, a petroleum engineer turned investment banker and possibly the most left-brained, practical guy she had ever met.

Marion convinced herself that her friend probably just needed some practice (since he was still studying this stuff), and she decided to lend him a shoulder. So, onward and upward to his apartment they went.

The healing table was centered on a red and beige oriental rug in the living room, covered with an itchy Navajo weaving. There was a side table with an assortment of tuning forks, small lights with different colored filters and vials of strange aromatic liquids. He first seemed to be waving his hands over her body, then clanged his tuning forks on his knee and made systematic circular motions over several parts of her body with his right hand. The colored lights were alternately in Philippe's left hand projecting a different color for each tuning fork he chose.

Amazing! In one hour, although he had barely physically touched her, Marion was able to move her arm normally without pain. Philippe had, however, touched her in a more profound way with his seemingly bizarre questions: What was the universe trying to communicate to her through pain and illness? Why was she ignoring her body? Didn't she know that her body was trying to tell her something? Frankly, Marion was stunned by these questions. But being very busy and now feeling better, her day-to-day life took precedence once again and she completely forgot his probing questions… until a few weeks later when for no apparent reason her other shoulder froze completely.

Back on Philippe's table soon thereafter, he said that if she didn't attend to answering the questions and finding out what she needed to learn, Marion would continue to experience symptoms. He explained that she had to understand what was going on in her heart and her mind in order to become more balanced. The prospect of further examining her emotional wellbeing was daunting. Marion had already spent four years in psychoanalysis four times a week with little sense of any greater personal awareness; and she had also sought other forms of psychotherapy on two continents to no avail in her pursuit for enlightenment. Philippe suggested that perhaps Marion should go to a place called Delphi. Motivated to end physical pain and get out of the rut she had found herself in, the real journey finally began.

Meanwhile, Tracy, in North Carolina, was leading a very busy life of her own trying to balance a thriving full-time private psychiatric practice and an active family life with three young children heavily involved in scouts, football, baseball and martial arts. She too was very much wrapped up in daily urban and professional life until a sequence of events suddenly threw her into a nightmare or -- as she sees it now with some perspective -- awakened her consciousness to the possibility that she too was stuck.

Her pain came in many forms. The first source of pain came from a former patient with borderline personality disorder who threatened a lawsuit, and Tracy discovered that her malpractice insurance carrier had filed for bankruptcy. The second form of pain arose from family health issues when her 2 year old twin niece required urgent open heart surgery; and at about the same time Tracy's sister was planning to donate 2/3 of her own liver to her spouse in a living donor transplant. Her sister wanted Tracy to go to New York to make all health decisions for her and her husband while they were both on life support. In addition, Tracy was experiencing increasing marital discord after 17 years of marriage; and she had just been told she had an abnormal mammogram. Her gynecologist and two radiologists informed her that "it would be too disfiguring" to biopsy all the spots and they recommended repeat mammograms every 3 months. It was the realization that Western medicine has its flaws and limitations along with the fact that she needed some inner peace that caused Tracy to pursue an alternative approach and training off the beaten path for herself... and for her patients.

During a chance lunch meeting a year earlier with a psychologist who had moved to town, she had heard of Delphi University. At the end of lunch he had mysteriously pulled Tracy aside and said in a hushed voice "I think you would like this place I went to once". He gave her the name and contact for Delphi, and he left without another word.

5

She promptly put the information away in her desk without another thought for 11 months... until the above series of events occurred.

When Tracy told her husband where she wanted to go and why, he informed her that he thought it sounded crazy. He exclaimed "why can't you just take some Prozac samples from your office and see if the angst goes away?!" So she made her first trek to Delphi with a good friend from her neighborhood with a pact that they would use the code words "Black Tennis Shoes" to signal that they should run for the hills without asking any questions in case, upon further scrutiny, they thought the place was some sort of cult.

Delphi University is tucked away in the hills outside of McCaysville, Georgia. It is difficult to find unless you are meant to be there—and an interesting place to say the least. Delphi is an Ancient Mystery School that holds classes in alternative and complementary healing, metaphysics, spiritual training, esoteric studies, transpersonal psychology and intuitive development. It was there that Tracy and Marion's paths first crossed, in a class at Delphi. As soon as Marion found out that Tracy was a physician (even worse, a psychiatrist!), she began recounting every psychiatrist and doctor joke she could think of with the sharpness and precision of a neurosurgeon. Despite the initial tension, a lasting friendship developed due to both women having a great desire to understand as much as possible regarding the ancient teachings and esoteric anatomy: the basis of disease and wellness (mental, emotional and physical).

The journey has truly been an awakening since completing instruction at Delphi and pursuing further training on other topics such as ancient healing mysteries, spiritual psychotherapy, traditional Chinese medicine, acupuncture with tuning forks, color and sound therapy (vibrational medicine), metaphysics, energy psychology, Reiki and other forms of energy healing. Tracy and Marion have each experienced a profound personal metamorphosis and grown into a new reality. The breast issue for Tracy has "completely disappeared" according to her gynecologist, two radiologists, a third repeat mammogram study, and a specialized 4-D breast MRI. Marion is now able to play golf once more and hike in the mountains of Peru.

Tracy and Marion began teaching regular weekend courses on how thoughts and feelings create obstacles or opportunities to enable us to either remain stuck or to manifest a sense of wellbeing in our lives. They have seen dramatic changes in the lives of their students who put the teachings to use on an ongoing basis. Several students as a result have changed or expanded careers, improved relationships, shifted health issues (some have gone into remission from chronic or acute illnesses), or even moved physical locations of their homes to other continents to pursue their dreams. Other students have experienced a profound sense of wellbeing despite the on-going challenges that spring up in their path. In essence, they have gotten unstuck in their lives in whatever form their "stuckness" took.

For example, Bob, a recent graduate of our course, is no longer emotionally paralyzed with fear after suffering for 15 years with Obsessive-Compulsive Disorder. He was afraid of germs and had an intense fear of developing cancer. He asked his wife to physically examine him at least 8 times a day for some form of cancer (usually skin or testicular). He was also afraid to travel to sunny places for fear of sun exposure and had deep anxiety about leaving his family to attend business meetings. The very next week after completing the course, he took his wife to the Bahamas, their first vacation in 10 years. In the first 3 months following his implementation of the tools he learned in the 12 Keys, his career TOOK OFF! His income tripled as he overcame his fear of contagion. He now travels to make sales presentations and has become more present in his daily life, as he is now able to get up close and personal, without germ phobia. He continues on medication for his psychiatric diagnosis but now the medication is working to control his symptoms to allow him to actually live. Prior to understanding and utilizing the concepts and techniques in the 12 Keys, Bob was barely existing and was experiencing fear and dread every day of his life on the same medications that he is on now. Many lives have been radically altered and enriched as a result of learning to apply the 12 Keys to Shift.

Reality and consciousness have shifted and been redefined for both of the authors and their students who put what they learn to use in their daily lives. They know how to get out of their stuck places by removing the obstacles that they assisted in attracting and creating in their lives. Marion and Tracy are still searching for more answers and are anxious to share with others what they have learned thus far in their journeys. They are writing this book in response to the questions from their friends, students, patients, family, colleagues and golf partners, as to how they have both dramatically changed in life style and priorities, seem much more at peace with themselves, more present in their own lives, and enjoy wonderful health.

This book includes their teachings and their combined wisdom to assist you with making a similar journey of your own if you so choose. This is the first book to give you daily practical techniques and tools to help you achieve and truly understand the 12 Keys to shift your life into gear and move forward.

Various Approaches to Healing Used in the 12 Keys:

This book brings together various practical, easy to use, complementary and integrative therapies and techniques to promote removal of unwanted, stagnant patterns in your life.

Meditation and Guided Imagery

Although meditation initially sprang up from Eastern religious or spiritual traditions, meditation techniques are described throughout history and have been used in many different cultures throughout the world for thousands of years. Today many people use meditation and its offshoot, guided imagery, for health and wellness purposes. Guided imagery is a directive form of meditation; whereas, classical meditation is done with focus on a specific breath technique, tone, concept, or mantra.

During meditation, a person learns to focus their attention and suspend the stream of thoughts that normally occupy and distract the mind (also known as brain chatter). This practice, which may also be combined with breathing techniques, is believed to result in a state of greater physical relaxation, decreased muscle tension, mental calmness, and psychological balance. Practicing meditation can change how a person relates and responds to the flow of emotions and thoughts in the mind.

Most types of meditation involve four components: 1) a quiet location with as few distractions as possible (with practice you may not require your surroundings to be quiet at all; however, this is helpful for beginners); 2) a comfortable posture (whether sitting, lying down, standing or walking); 3) a specific focus of attention; and 4) an open mind (letting distractions come and go without judgment or analysis and gently returning the attention to the meditation).

Mindfulness- The 2500-year-old Method of Introspection

How can such a simple concept be so powerful? Mindfulness, a philosophy as well as a type of meditation, can free up our thoughts to enable us to experience the richness of the moment. How many of us remember what we did yesterday, much less last week? We are either so busy rushing around on autopilot, focusing on deadlines and thinking about past and future events, that we never actually stop and are fully present in the experience of the moment. Mindfulness opens up our awareness to experience, observe and accept things as they are, without judgment. It's not about withdrawing from your emotions or banishing all of your thoughts. It teaches us how to embrace reality by stilling our busy, anxious and restless minds. It enables us to quiet our anxieties, unwanted feelings and self-critical thoughts.

In this book we will teach you how to use mindfulness in a meditation practice. The National Institutes of Health now have a CAM (Complementary and Alternative Medicine) website at www.nccam. nih.gov that describes the documented benefits of meditation as a mind-body technique for physical and emotional wellness.

Vibrational Healing (Color and Sound Therapy)

The primary healing modality used in ancient Greece and Egypt was vibrational healing – healing with color and sound. Certain vibrational frequencies are embodied in specific colors, musical notes and the vibration of the human voice.

There are 7 principal energy centers in the body often referred to as chakras in eastern tradition, each of which when in a state of wellness reflect and vibrate to a characteristic color, tone and musical note. When this vibration shifts out of balance, there is the creation of dissonance that may manifest as mental, emotional or physical disarray. Utilizing specific sounds, musical tones or colors (through intention, the appropriately colored garment or colored light) can assist with rebalancing the energy centers and restoring wellness. Richard Gerber, M.D. does an excellent job of describing the use of various colors for healing proposed by different researchers and practitioners in his book A Practical Guide to Vibrational Medicine. There is also a very helpful website (one of our favorites on the chakra system) at www.healer. ch/ChakraRefEnglish.pdf created by the Brofman Foundation for the Advancement of Healing that concisely relates colors and specific musical notes with areas of the body.

Traditional Chinese Medicine: Life force energy and meridians

Chinese call life force energy *chi* (or *qi*), also known as *prana* in India and *ki* in Japan. It is the cause for all vital movement within the body. This concept of life energy is rooted in a 5,000-year-old tradition of Chinese philosophy and medicine, based on the belief of the existence of energy channels carrying vital life force to the internal organs. There are 12 primary meridians that pass through a number of body organs for which they are named and then 8 extraordinary meridians, which collect, store and distribute energy throughout the body. These energy flow circuits do not correspond with any physical structures described in Western medicine teachings, such as arteries, veins or nerves. These energy pathways were mapped out independently in both China and India as far back as 1000 BC.

More people have used acupuncture than any other system of medicine throughout history. According to the National Institutes of Health, preclinical studies have documented acupuncture's effects, but they have not been able to comprehend how acupuncture works within the framework of the Western system of medicine. That is because acupuncture works on the body's subtle energy system rather than directly on the physical body (see Dr. Richard Gerber's book, A Practical Guide to Vibrational Medicine). Stimulating a particular acupoint (acupuncture point) within a meridian line on a body affects the energy movement along that specific meridian pathway and can assist with releasing blocks and rebalancing energy flow. Acupoints can be stimulated by tapping, twisting, needles, holding, color, sound (musical notes or toning), and/or focused intention.

The basis for tapping on meridians for enhancement of wellness is becoming increasingly recognized today through the efforts of pioneers in the field such as George Goodheart, Dr. Roger Callahan, John Diamond, Gary Craig and Fred Gallo. Several systems for tapping on energy points have been taught widely since the 1980s and include: Energy Diagnostic and Treatment Methods, Emotional Freedom Technique, Thought Field Therapy, and Tapas Acupressure Technique. The fields of Energy Medicine and Energy Psychology are growing rapidly in the United States and around the world.

Tapping techniques can assist us in freeing ourselves from negative emotions, faulty thoughts and physical ailments that may have kept us stuck in emotional, physical, mental and spiritual scenarios in our life. All the tapping techniques presented in this book involve only a bit of gentle tapping on specific points, affirmations, counting, humming and eye movements along with a genuine intention to shift the problem, thought or emotion. Tapping techniques can sometimes rapidly shift a thought, feeling or issue that might otherwise take months or years to shift in traditional therapeutic processes.

Our aim is to give you a brief introduction to this wonderful concept of energy medicine, because the solutions to our problems are often found within our body, as well as our mind and spirit. For those of you interested in delving further into this topic, we highly recommend the book entitled Energy Medicine by Donna Eden and David Feinstein. In our book we will often use the tapping technique known as the Emotional Freedom Technique (EFT) developed by Gary Craig, as well as a mix of other energy psychology protocols. The EFT techniques we will use in this book are outlined in detail in Key 1.

KEY 1. The Obstacle of Feeling Unloved

Remember that old childhood rhyming song: "Nobody likes me. Everybody hates me. Guess I'll go eat worms...?" We all have had one of those days where we felt utterly unloved and unlovable. It is so human. It may be because of something we did or something someone else did to us, or perhaps it may be due to life circumstances where we felt that no one recognized our accomplishments or abilities. Perhaps we are just feeling lonely and disconnected from everyone; or we feel guilty about something we did to someone else and, therefore, believe ourselves to be unworthy of love. We question how anyone could possibly love someone as awful as me?

When we feel this way, it appears that nothing will go right for us. We live with the perception of lack and futility. We can't see or experience anything but lack and futility in our lives when that is all that we open ourselves to perceive. There seems to be no joy in our life, and abundance escapes us when we harbor thoughts that we are not loved. There is no passion in our relationships, work, hobbies or activities that usually fulfill us. We feel empty. In essence, we are empty. We are stuck in our perception of emptiness, isolation, and lack of belonging or connectedness to someone or something.

What gets in the way of feeling lovable?
- Negative life experiences both past and present (poor health, abusive relationships, traumatic experiences)
- Negative parental influence (judgmental statements from childhood that have been internalized such as "You will never

amount to anything", "You are bad", "You can't do anything right", "You ruined my life")

- Grief and loss (of persons, pets, social status, occupation, power, relationships, health, or possessions)
- Guilt (over past action or inaction imagined or real that is now regretted)
- Abandonment (by parents/spouses through separation or divorce, by friends/loved ones through life circumstances or relocation, by God)
- Unworthiness (sense of being "less than" others due to past experiences)
- Shame (of what we perceive was done by us or to us in the past)
- Embarrassment (of physical appearance, social status, actions, life experiences)
- Loneliness (sense of isolation or lack of connection to anyone)
- Rejection (in relationships, at work or school)
- Culture or Creed creating separation (division by race, belief, sex, groups, teams, our competitive nature, socioeconomic status, education, preferences, religious dogma)

We are always creating separation by either thinking of ourselves as being included in or excluded from groups or situations. We judge our selves and others at times by what groups we associate ourselves with or what possessions we have or don't have. Think of how often we have met someone and asked: "Where do you live?" "What school did you go to?" "What team do you root for?" "What car do you drive?" Think of how often we strive to "keep up with the Joneses down the street" for fear of being judged or for how we judge ourselves if we do not have equal status symbols to those we admire. We essentially judge ourselves by how we believe we appear to others (physical appearance), our possessions, and our apparent attitudes (thoughts and feelings) rather than by whom we really are.

Many people perceive themselves to be nothing more than their physical body, thoughts and feelings. When we do this, we feel alone and isolated in handling our daily stresses and challenges in life. We do not understand that we are part of a greater whole and we take everything personally that occurs in our daily life. We begin to create a feedback loop (see Figure 1) based on how our body responds to stressors and the thoughts and emotions that are triggered by the stressors from our past experiences. It is easy to get lost in this repetitive pattern of our thoughts and feelings that get dredged up. We feel trapped with no exit.

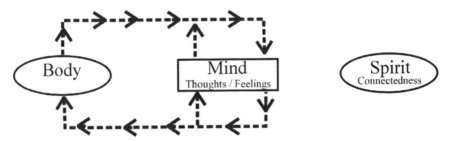

Let's consider a scenario where we see this feedback loop in action. For example, something as simple as a trip to the store can rapidly trap us in a spiral of faulty thoughts that isolates us in a world of our own creation.

Imagine that you are driving to a major shopping center in the height of the holiday season to make some last minute purchases. You have somehow deluded yourself to believe that you will be the only person who will be making such a last minute visit to this store and that you will likely just breeze in and out in ten minutes. As you pull into the packed parking lot, you spy a parking space opening up just in the front of the store's entrance. What luck! You pull close to the space, turning on your blinker to indicate to the world that this space is YOURS. As you begin to contentedly hum a cheery tune, you wait patiently as the person currently occupying the space begins to back out. Everything is going according to plan and you will be home in time for dinner.

However, as you sit there imagining how good dinner will taste, a small green VW bug zips into your parking space before you can maneuver into it. The outrage of this injustice begins to boil within you. You feel your muscles getting tense as you tighten your grip on the steering wheel. As you clench your jaw, you begin to think "Why does this always happen to me?!" Feeling angry and like a victim, thoughts resurface from earlier in the day at work and begin to flood into your mind. "The boss overlooked me again for the promotion." "Someone else got the credit for the successful project that I did". "Nobody appreciates me!"

You begin to chew on the bones that have been buried in the recesses of your subconscious. "Nothing ever goes my way." "I am never good enough for anyone to notice." "I may as well be invisible!" "I will fail at everything I do!" The acid begins to churn in your stomach as your blood pressure rises, your head begins to pound and your jaw tightens further. "I think I am having a heart attack!!" "Wait until I find that jerk with the VW bug and give him a piece of my mind!" Your anxiety begins to turn into panic as you are becoming convinced that you are indeed experiencing symptoms of a heart attack since that does run in your family.

"Didn't Aunt Martha have a heart attack at age 46?!" Increasingly breathless, you look distractedly for another parking space as your mind chews more profoundly on the faulty thoughts from the past that are being unearthed at a frighteningly fast pace. After several minutes you finally find a space that is in the outermost edge of the parking lot. You can almost see in the distance the front of the store (if you had the binoculars you were planning on purchasing) from where you are now parked and you know that it will take ten minutes to make the trek to the entrance in the cold and now drizzly weather. As you trudge to the store cursing under your breath, you barely even notice the extremely pregnant, exhausted young woman with two toddlers trailing behind the brimming shopping cart that she is pushing in the rain. You are so lost in your own negative thoughts and feelings of anxiety, anger and resentment that you do not even notice the car heading for the last trailing child.

In the above scenario, you are feeling unlovable, terribly alone, disconnected, victimized, angry and panicked as you become adversely physically affected and isolated by your thoughts and feelings. You take everything going on around you personally. How could you have possibly dealt with the above scenario in a different manner? What is the key that will unlock the repetitive cycle of thoughts and emotions that results in physical symptoms and isolation? How can you create anew?

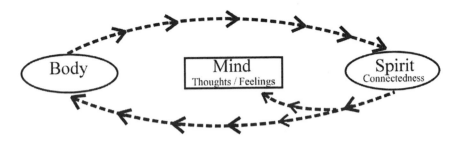

Imagine once again that you are headed to that major shopping center at the height of the holiday season, still searching for that convenient, close parking space and looking forward to returning home soon for dinner. You spot the space at the store entrance that is about to become available. Once again you indicate to the world that you are about to make this spot your very own. However, right on cue, here comes the green VW bug whipping into the space ahead of you while you dream of your scrumptious meal awaiting you at home.

You feel that all too human and ego-based flash of anger and resentment from the injustice of the situation, but this time you deal with it from an evolved mindset. This time you do not take it personally. When you get out of a victim mentality and become the observer of people and situations in the world around you, you take on a whole different perspective. Once you transform the anger and resentment (see Key 4) about losing the coveted parking space, you remind yourself that we are all part of a greater whole.

Perhaps the person driving the VW bug had a real need to be closer to the entrance; they might be handicapped or have a sick child at home or some other greater need for having that space. Or perhaps we are needed elsewhere at that moment. It is not always just about us. We drive on looking for another spot and finally find the one out in the nether regions of the lot. When we get out of the car, we are not caught in the loop of how we feel we are victims of circumstances or other people's actions, so instead of being caught in our own internal loop of faulty thoughts and emotional reactions, we are fully present and in the moment. We feel part of a greater whole.

That is when we notice the very pregnant, exhausted young mother and her two toddlers. We observe that she is not fully present to monitor her own children's safety as a car is rapidly approaching. This time we are no longer self-absorbed. We are fully present and available to quickly rescue her child from danger. From this perspective we become acutely aware that everything occurs for a reason even though we might not understand it fully in the moment. There is a reason for every circumstance and every person who crosses our paths. Every lost parking space and, in fact, every encounter becomes a new adventure and opportunity.

The missing piece from the first scenario is that there is no connection to spirit (which we define as god, source, universe, collective consciousness, higher power, chi) or unity with one another (see Figure 2). When you feel disconnected from a sense of a greater whole, everything that occurs in your life centers on you. You perceive that you are alone in the world and you are nothing more than your physical body, thoughts and emotions. This tends to breed the mentality that "whoever has the most toys in the end wins". It is "kill or be killed". There isn't enough for everyone. Competition is everywhere and you see everyone as a potential competitor.

When you add spirit or a sense of connectedness to others into the mix and feel the connection, your whole awareness and consciousness shift. You focus your attention on being part of a greater whole in which you play a vital role. You become aware that you are important and have a purpose in this great experience of life. It is not about being a victim. What is going on around you transcends you as an individual at every moment and yet involves your participation.

It is important to recall and be aware daily that you are loved and lovable at all times no matter what is going on in your life: You are never alone or abandoned. There is never an actual separation between us and any other person or thing. When you consider that each of us are energetic or spiritual beings residing in and expressing through a physical body, then you understand that there is no separation between energy/spirit and matter. When you have this awareness, there is never a sense of abandonment. You experience a sense of connectedness in knowing that All are One, and One are Many. We are all part of the bigger whole.

For instance, have you ever had the experience of suddenly thinking of someone and then they call you on the phone, show up on your doorstep, or you run into them at the most unlikely place soon thereafter? Have you ever had a strong feeling that a child or loved one was in trouble or in great need only to find out later that your intuition was correct? We are energetically connected to our loved ones at all times.... And they are connected to us as well. You just need to tune in. Your loved ones are constantly sending you love every moment, and all you need do is to take the time to be mindfully aware of and experience their love flowing to you in order to feel it.

What about those times where you have had a falling out with a loved one? Even though we become angry at one another over situations at times, there is still a deeper, underlying connection and love for that person that remains. Do you recall that, perhaps even after a breakup or a misunderstanding that causes the end of a close relationship, you might sense that there will always be a place in your heart beyond the hurt for that person even though you may not choose to have an on-going intimate relationship with them? This is because we are energetically connected to one another and when we can transform our anger, resentment, or shame, we can allow ourselves to feel love and compassion, become aware, and shift our perceptions. The following meditation and exercises will assist you with becoming aware of and experiencing this love and connectedness to others.

Exercises for When You Feel Alone, Unloved or Unlovable:

1. Loved Ones Meditation:
Hint- This meditation will be more effective if you have a friend read it with feeling to you or you record yourself reading it with heart on an audio tape and play it back to follow as you meditate in a quiet private space. This meditation can also be found on a companion CD that accompanies this book (for details see <u>www.12keystoshift.com</u>).

Close your eyes. Take a deep breath and as you exhale feel all of your tension releasing from your body. Take two more slow deep breaths and each time you exhale, feel your muscles relaxing more and more.

Feel yourself walking on a soft, green mossy path in the countryside. It's an enjoyable spring day filled with the sounds of nature. The warmth of the radiant sun fills the air and your eyes delight in the beauty of nature. You are on your own special journey and it feels so nurturing to have some time for yourself. As you walk on the path, you are guided to a gently sloping field with wildflowers and every imaginable variety of colorful, vibrant butterflies. They are everywhere, fluttering, floating and alighting on the wildflowers. Feel the perfection of all this beauty.

Stop for a moment and allow yourself to fully absorb the scene. Allow it to permeate all of your senses. As you observe the scene more closely, one special butterfly will draw your attention. (Pause) Focus on this one butterfly. Take in its brilliant form and color. As you marvel at its beauty, the butterfly begins to transform. While you continue to watch the butterfly, it transforms into one of your loved ones. Your loved one is now standing there in the field surrounded by beautiful butterflies. Feel your love gently streaming towards your loved one and feel their love flowing toward you. The gentle peace of their love embraces you and feels so good. Be aware of the love flowing back and forth between you healing and dissolving any and all past relationship strife, which has come between you.

As you remain focused on the field and all of its vibrant beauty, the butterflies begin to transform into all of those people dear to your heart. There are so many butterflies and they continue to transform. Now they are transforming into all of the special people in your past that have brought inspiration into your life. Watch in wonder as they appear before you. Express your love and gratitude to them all for enriching your life. Feel your love expanding outward and enveloping them all, and feel their love flowing toward you.

Know that your loved ones are constantly sending you love at every moment. You may return to this field at any time to feel the warmth of love and to spend time with or communicate with those who are dear to your heart. When you are ready to return from this beautiful meadow filled with loved ones, feel yourself slowly returning to your body and gently open your eyes.

2. Loving Benefactor Exercise:

Find a comfortable, seated position on a chair or cushion and allow your body to settle into position. Close your eyes and begin to focus your attention on your breath, following your cycles of inhalation and exhalation. Notice the rising and falling sensations on your belly as you breathe in and out and follow this for a few cycles.

Now try to bring to mind a heartfelt sense or visual image of someone whom you believe embodies the qualities of unconditional love and compassion. This person can be a friend or relative, a religious or historical figure, a spiritual being or just someone who embodies these qualities. Picture this person as if they were sitting or standing right in front of you.

Look into their eyes and feel the absolute unconditional love and compassion flowing from them towards you. Now radiate feelings of love and gratitude back towards this person. Whenever you feel your mind wandering, gently bring your attention back to the image of the loving friend, historical or spiritual image and once again practice radiating love, empathy and compassion towards them. Feel their love, empathy and compassion radiating back towards you.

Stay with your Loving Benefactor and feel their love flowing to you and your love flowing to them for up to 20 minutes. Know that this Loving Benefactor is sending you love every minute of every day.

3. Root Chakra Exercise:

The root chakra is located in front of the body at the level of the pubic bone. This chakra has to do with our feelings of safety and security in the world. It is also about belonging in the physical world. It is believed that this chakra resonates with the color red, the tone "uh" (as in the vowel sound in "cup"), and the musical notes of C or F (whichever resonates more strongly with you).

Get into a comfortable seated position on a chair with your spine erect and your feet flat on the floor. Gently close your eyes. Take a few deep, relaxing breaths and with each out breath feel your muscles progressively relaxing.

Now visualize, sense or feel the bottom of your feet connecting with the earth. Become aware of how powerful and safe you feel with your feet firmly connected to the energy of Mother Earth. Sense the loving energy and strength from the earth moving slowly up your legs and into your root chakra. Visualize, sense or feel your root chakra being filled with the color red swirling in a circular motion. Your root chakra becomes more vital and energized as it fills with this beautiful red swirling energy and all negativity is removed.

Take a deep breath and as you exhale tone out loud "uh". Tone in this manner seven times and notice the vibration of the tone within your root chakra. Be aware of how safe and secure you feel connected to the earth and everyone and everything. Remain connected to this loving, vibrant, safe energy for 3 to 5 minutes. As you slowly bring your focus back to your physical surroundings, continue to feel your connection to the earth and to everything. Be mindful of this connection as you go about the activities of your day or as you drift off to sleep at night.

Note: If you have a piano or tuning forks or another musical instrument available to you, you may also add into the above exercise striking and holding the corresponding musical note at the same time as you tone the vowel sound.

4. Energy Medicine Techniques:
A. Self care protocol (Also known as The 3 Thumps as presented by Donna Eden in her book <u>Energy Medicine</u>)

This routine comes from the ancient Chinese method of balancing the energy flow of the body by tapping on acupuncture meridians.

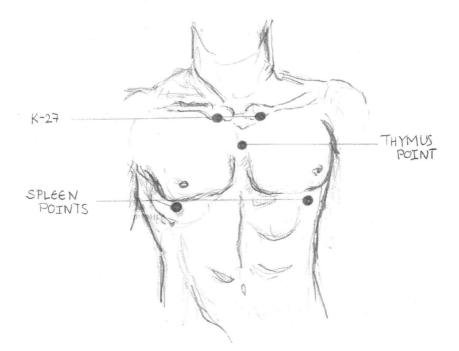

Tap each point for 30 seconds

Tap the K-27 points under the collarbone near the sternum or breastbone. This is the top point of the kidney meridian. This is a great point for keeping your energies moving forward, energizing your body and improving focus.

Tap the thymus point in the sternum to stimulate the immune system and boost your vitality. This point is found in the following manner: Lightly place your index fingertip at the top of your breastbone (below the Adam's apple). Now slowly trace your fingertip downwards approximately 2 to 2 1/2 inches and you will notice that there is a slight bony bulge. You are now at the level of the thymus.

Tap the spleen point under your breasts to energize and balance the body's energy system. In men this point may be found approximately 3 inches below the nipple. In women this point may be found mid-nipple line, approximately one thumb's width below where the wire of an underwire bra would lay against the body.

B. EFT Protocol

In every key we describe various energy medicine techniques. While we often recommend the use of EFT to assist with shifting limiting thoughts, it is important to note that this is NOT a book about EFT. We are giving the reader a relatively basic technique specific to the issue in each key. If you are interested in pursuing a more comprehensive understanding of EFT and its various uses, then we suggest you check out the increasingly abundant literature on this wonderful technique. Gary Craig at his website www.emofree.com has several links to almost any application of this method imaginable. He also sells DVDs at a reasonable price.

Before we fully describe the EFT technique, let's review some points to maximize the results of energy therapy.

1. **Hydrate:** Drink water as we are working with our body's electromagnetic energy. Water is the best conductor of electrical energy, so it is essential to drink before energy treatments.

2. **Correction for Excess Energy:**

Our imbalance in the meridians can come from being over-charged and having too much energy. This results in feeling spaced out, confused or overwhelmed. To correct for over-energy: Cross the left ankle over the right ankle, extend arms with backs of hands facing each other, bring right hand over left, clasp fingers together, fold arms and hands inward and rest the hands on the chest under the chin; place your tongue on the roof of your mouth behind your front teeth, breathe deeply for 1-2 minutes. It's very calming for most individuals and can be used as a separate exercise to promote sleep and reduce acute anxiety.

Psychological Reversal: A Psychological Reversal (PR) is when conflict outside of your awareness interferes with your desire to pursue your conscious intention. You are acting in opposition to what you are consciously trying to obtain. Example, if you were asked if you want to be joyful, the expected response would be "yes", but experience has proven that when people are psychologically reversed that they self-sabotage; they perhaps would respond yes but actually unconsciously choose to be miserable for reasons outside of their awareness. Perhaps they don't deeply feel that they deserve to be joyful due to feelings of guilt, unworthiness, shame, etc. Thus, there is a conflict between internal beliefs and what one desires to achieve. An energy reversal blocks your ability to see solutions even when you have the knowledge, or it prevents you from implementing the solution even though you have the ability. When you have a goal that triggers a PR, effectiveness of the treatment will be hindered until the PR is resolved. Tapping neutralizes most PRs quickly. When a PR is present, the first step is to state that you completely accept yourself with all your flaws including the problem is that is causing you distress.

Treating Reversals: Reversals can be dealt with almost instantaneously with the following procedure. The remedy involves repeating an affirmation three times, combined with tapping or rubbing on an energy point. Define the problem and create an affirmation that corresponds to it. Begin with "Even though I have this ------, I deeply and completely accept myself with all my feelings." The affirmation should dissolve the problem.

Some examples to fill in the blank:

"Even though I feel so depressed, I deeply and completely accept myself with all my feelings."

" Even though I have this: fear of bees, craving for cigarettes, pain in my shoulder, anger towards my boss, traumatic childhood memory, nightmares, etc., I deeply and completely love and accept myself with all my feelings."

For the affirmation to be effective, acknowledge the problem and create self-acceptance in spite of the problem. Whether you believe the affirmation or not does not matter. Say it with feeling and out loud while tapping the karate chop (KC) point with the fingertips of the opposite hand. The KC point is that part of your hand that you would use to deliver a karate chop (between top of wrist and the base of the pinky finger). (For a diagram depicting the KC point, see Figure 5 under Basic Tapping Protocol later in this Key.) Repeat the affirmation 3 times while tapping on the KC point. Don't forget to breathe and feel the affirmation in your heart center.

Now we are ready to learn what Gary Craig, founder of EFT, calls the Basic Recipe, where we tap near the end points of several energy meridians to diminish the intensity of almost any problem. The Basic Recipe consists of The Setup, The Sequence, The 9 Gamut Procedure, The Sequence (again), The Reminder Phrase, and adjustments for subsequent rounds of tapping.

1. Start by doing a balancing procedure (the energy self care routine, 3 thumps, connecting central and governing meridians). See the exercises in Appendix.

2. Identify and clearly state a target problem. The target problem can be anything that causes emotional or physical distress.

3. Focus on the target problem and rate the intensity of distress on a scale from 0 (no problem) to 10 (worst imaginable), Write down the number ranking your level of distress when you think about the problem.

4. Perform the PR correction maneuver by tapping on the KC point and stating 3 times " Even though I have this... I deeply and completely love and accept myself with all my feelings."

5. Create a reminder phrase which will be a word or short phrase to assist you with remaining attuned to the problem while you are performing the following tapping sequence. Examples include: "fear of heights", fear of public speaking", "craving for alcohol", "anger at my father", "pain in my back", "anxiety at recalling traumatic event".

6. **Basic Tapping Protocol:**
The tapping sequence we are going to describe is a modification from the original EFT protocol. As Gary Craig, pointed out in his EFT manual (a free download is on line at www.emofree.com), stimulation of only a few points on each major meridian is usually necessary because the meridians are interconnected and stimulating one meridian will most probably affect others. A variety of sequences can be used. The protocol we teach involves tapping on eight points. Below are the abbreviations for the eight tapping points. These are summarized in the same order as they are presented in Figure 5 and in the Appendix.

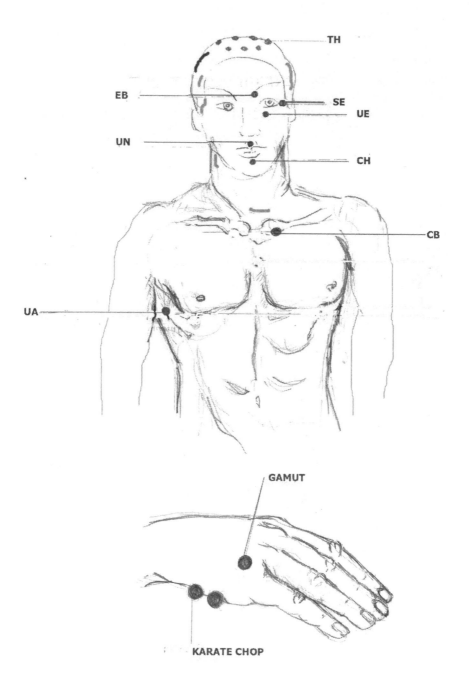

1. EB (for "Eyebrow") is at the edge of the eyebrow, just inside and above the bridge of the nose.
2. SE (for "Side of the Eye") is on the bone bordering the outer edge of the eye.
3. UE (for "Under the Eye") is on the bone under either eye, about one inch below the pupil.
4. UN (for "Under the Nose") is on the area between the nose and the top of the upper lip.
5. Ch (for "Chin") is midway between the point of the chin and the bottom of the lower lip.
6. CB (for "Collarbone") is just below the junction where the sternum (breastbone), collarbone, and the first rib meet (you learned this point earlier as "K-27").
7. UA (for "Under the Arm") is about four inches below the armpit, about even with the nipple for men, or in the middle of the bra strap for women.
8. TH (for the "Top of the Head") is a series of points in a circle as if one was wearing a crown on top of the head.

Tap with either hand, or both hands simultaneously. You can tap with 2 or 3 fingertips. Tap firmly yet gently without hurting or bruising the body.

Tap approximately seven times on each point. Most acupoints exist on both sides of the body, so it doesn't matter which side you tap on. You can experiment and see if one side is more effective than another or tap on both sides simultaneously. Remember that you should be mindfully repeating the reminder phrase while you are tapping on the above points.

When you have completed these steps, once more assess the intensity of the problem: Close your eyes, focus on the original problem or issue, and rank it from 0 to 10 for the amount of distress it now causes you. If there is no trace whatsoever of your previous emotional or physical distress, then your work with this issue is completed.

If only partial relief is obtained, additional rounds may be necessary. Two simple adjustments need to be made for these subsequent rounds.

1. **Psychological Reversals:** A possible obstacle to success during the first round of treatment is the re-emergence of psychological reversals in a different form. After treatment has begun and some progress has been made, the psychological reversal takes on a subtly different quality. It is no longer preventing any change in the condition being treated, but it may be hindering further progress. It is important that the wording of the new affirmation take into account the fact that some progress has been made. The addition of two simple words accomplishes this:

"Even though I still have some of this _____, I deeply love and accept myself with all my feelings."

The words 'still' and 'some' changes the emphasis of the affirmation toward a focus on the remainder of the problem. The sample affirmation below reflects an adjustment to the affirmations listed earlier:

"Even though I still have some of this fear of spiders, I deeply love and accept myself with all my feelings".

2. The Reminder Phrase also needs a minor adjustment by placing the word 'remaining' in the original reminder phrase:

"This remaining fear of large spiders" (or simply "remaining fear")

Following each round, do a new 0 to 10 ranking of the level of distress you now feel when you tune into the original problem. If the level of distress continues to decrease, do further rounds until you reach 0, or until the distress stops decreasing.

The 9 Gamut Procedure: This procedure is only necessary if you are having difficulty in decreasing your level of distress, after 2 or more rounds of the basic procedure. Roger Callahan's 9 Gamut Procedure is one of the more strange-looking procedures in EFT, with the tapping, eye movements, humming, and counting all designed to stimulate and connect specific parts of the brain. It takes only 10 seconds to complete; yet it makes EFT more efficient and speeds up your progress towards emotional freedom, especially if sandwiched between two complete rounds of the 8-point protocol.

In the 9 Gamut Procedure, you must first locate the gamut point on the back of either hand, 1/2 inch beyond the knuckles (toward the wrist), and in line with the midpoint between the pinky finger and the ring finger. (All tapping points, including the gamut point are pictured in Figure 5 as well as in the Appendix.) While constantly tapping the gamut point, do the following nine actions:

1. Close eyes.
2. Open eyes.
3. While holding the head still, shift eyes to lower left.
4. While holding head still, move eyes to lower right.
5. Roll eyes clockwise 360 degrees while keeping head still.
6. Roll eyes counter-clockwise 360 degrees while holding head still.
7. Hum a few bars of your favorite tune for a few seconds (e.g., "Somewhere Over the Rainbow", "Happy Birthday," "Row, Row Your Boat.")
8. Count to five.
9. Hum once again.

For a synopsis of this EFT protocol, we recommend that you download the EFT manual from the internet at the above-mentioned address and examine page 40 of Gary Craig's manual.

Example EFT Phrases Pertaining To Feeling Unloved:

"Even though I feel so different from everyone else because_____ (fill in the blank) and can't imagine ever feeling loved, I deeply love and accept myself with all my feelings."

"Even though I feel so unlovable because I have been abandoned by __ ____(fill in the blank) and if they couldn't love me why should anyone else, I choose to deeply love and accept myself with all these feelings anyway."

" Even though I am so bad that I don't deserve love, I deeply love and accept myself with all these awful feelings."

"Even though my body isn't what I want it to be and it embarrasses me, I deeply love and accept myself with all my feelings."

"Even though I feel like I am what I do, hate what I do and have no self respect, I deeply love and accept myself with all my feelings."

"Even though I feel I am what I do and right now I am not working/ doing anything, I deeply love and accept myself with all my feelings."

"Even though I feel so invisible and unimportant that I can't understand how anyone could love me, I deeply and completely love and accept myself with all these negative feelings."

Affirmations

The internal chatter that goes on in your head daily serves as your own dogma which limits you in what you believe is possible to create or manifest in your life. It can make you stuck. It develops your own personal mind-set, the way you perceive the world. This internal dogma creates a potential personal prison that dictates what you are able to accomplish, how you think you need to appear, whether you are able to love self or others. It defines what your material and physical comfort levels should be, your opportunities, limitations, and critical judgments of self/others; and generally determines who you think you are. These have become your truths, your true affirmations learned through your experiences and perceptions.

In order to shift your internal dogma, you must first become aware of your world in a different way. We energize what we think about and focus on. What do you tend to focus on? Once you become aware of the limiting thoughts that you have, you are well into the first step of transforming that personal dogma which is keeping you from experiencing more joy in your life. Knowing and acknowledging the faulty thought is the key to unlocking the door of your prison. When you are ready to let go of an old faulty thought that has been limiting you in some fashion, affirmations can be a powerful way of energizing a new perception of the world and your life.

Affirmations do work, as long as they do not conflict with a more tightly held current dogma or your powerful subconscious thoughts.

Understand that your self-talk can potentially be a huge obstacle to overriding a new affirmation. For example, if your affirmation is " I am free to love and be loved" and after you repeat this a few times you hear your internal chatter suggesting "yes but who could ever love someone as ugly as me" or "yes but if someone loves me there must be something wrong with them", or "yes but why would anyone want to love someone as angry, fat, etc. as me?" You get the picture? Gary Craig calls these "tail-enders". A tail-ender describes a scenario where you completely unwittingly negate the intention of your affirmation with the stronger intention of your internal dogma.

With EFT tapping we can change our consistent unwanted thoughts and create a new reality in our energy system, once we are able to become aware of the prison that we have locked our self in. The combination of affirmations and EFT can powerfully assist us in redesigning our mind set and energy system. We can observe all the negative self talk (the yes buts...) that come up after we state the affirmations and tap away at the conflicting beliefs, hidden fears, subconscious scripts and negative emotions to clear ourselves prior to installing the new.

The helpful guidelines below for constructing affirmations have been suggested by Gary Craig on the www.emofree.com website.

1. You must affirm a WANT and not a SHOULD.
It has to be a very meaningful goal, which is coming from your own heartfelt desire, not what you perceive your family or society expects of you.

2. You must affirm your 'wants' and not your 'don't wants'. Your subconscious mind does not know the difference between yes and no. When it is a weight affirmation, for example, don't say, " I don't want to be fat". The focus will only be on the negative issue of "the fat" and will continually energize that. As an alternative, try "My normal weight is 122 pounds and that is what I weigh". Another affirmation example might be concerning golf. When you address the ball, you affirm that you want to drive the ball down the middle of the fairway, you don't say "don't go into the bunker!" or "don't go into the lake!" Otherwise your focus is on the sand and the water. Visualization is very powerful. Visualize the positive outcome and energize that instead of

the negative. Why waste energy on creating more negative outcomes in your life?

3. You must believe that your goal is realistically possible. The goals you set must be reachable within your own system of belief or mind set. Your imagination and belief is the most powerful tool you have to create in your life. If you cannot imagine it, you cannot create it.

4. Your goals must be a "stretch" and big enough to be exciting. Otherwise, you will soon be bored repeating the affirmation and will not be energizing it as strongly. They also must be a stretch beyond your current limits to create excitement about the affirmation. As you begin to create anew in your life, you will become aware and amazed at how deeply constrained your life was due to your past faulty thoughts.

5. The affirmation must be stated in the first person, present tense. You are using the statement to program your intention. It doesn't have to be true when you say it. You may be feeling ill and state that "I am in wonderful health". "I will be in wonderful health soon," won't get you there. Soon may never arrive. When you create with the idea that the moment for change is in the future, you create that it is ALWAYS in the future and NEVER in the present.

6. Augment your affirmation with daydreams. Present tense daydreams can be THE most powerful tool for establishing new consistent thoughts. The brain cannot differentiate what is real from what is strongly imagined. So imagine who you want to be and what you want to do and program your beliefs. When you visualize it intensely, over time your brain will catch up and you can recreate yourself. Athletes often do this to enhance their sports performance.

7. Do not affirm the actions of other people. You cannot create for someone else, only for yourself. Use, "I attract others because I am a warm, loving person", not "Jim loves me."

8. Keep your affirmations private. Announcing them to others often invites criticisms and judgment.

Procedure for Tapping Regarding Affirmations:

1. Identify and clearly state your sincere affirmation.
2. Then target the "tail-ender" or "yes, but" phrase linked to your affirmation that can encompass emotional or physical reactions.
3. Rate the intensity of the distress level caused by the "tail-ender" on a scale from 0-10. Write down the number indicating the amount of distress you experience when you think about the problem.
4. Perform the appropriate PR correction maneuver.
5. Create a reminder phrase.
6. Perform the Basic 8 Point Tapping Protocol for the "tail-ender" issues. Make certain you cover every "yes, but" linked to your affirmation.

After you have completed the above procedure for all "tail-enders" to your affirmation, you now tap in your positive affirmation. When you tap in a positive affirmation, you start with tapping on your third eye or the point in the middle of your forehead. You may also choose, if you so desire, to tap in the affirmation at each of the 8 tapping points.

6. Applying Key 1:

Example 1: Greg was a 50-year-old male with severe generalized anxiety. He had quite an abusive childhood with a father who was extremely violent --primarily toward his mother but also toward Greg. His mother died recently after battling a long debilitating neurological illness exacerbated by his father's physical abuse of her. He had promised his mother on her deathbed that he would "take care of" his father who continued to be extremely verbally and emotionally abusive of Greg. Even though Greg lives far away from his father and has been successful in his business, he is transported back to his wounded child whenever he speaks with his father, which has been more frequently since his mother's death.

He came to my office distressed from memories of his childhood relating to his father's abuse. Traditional psychotherapy had given him minimal shifting of his long-standing shadow thought from childhood that he was unlovable (as a child always just wants love and acceptance from his or her parents no matter how abusive the parent is to the child). I asked if he would be willing to try a different approach in dealing with his traumatic memories. He was agreeable although somewhat skeptical.

We utilized the 8-point EFT protocol described above for the faulty thought "I am unlovable/I deserve what I got". He started out at a distress level of 9 by his report and after going through the protocol the first time the level of distress dropped down to a 3. I had him repeat the protocol and he reported a ranking of a "1" by the end of the second round. He was very pleased with the response and reported significant relief. He continues to use these techniques regularly to deal with on-going intermittent contact with his father.

Example 2: Joel was a 50-year-old male in the process of trying to decide if he had to pursue competency issues with his progressively demented elderly father. He was commuting from Charlotte, North Carolina to Charleston, South Carolina frequently to care for his father and it was creating tremendous stress for both he and his wife. He had much anxiety over the effect the stress was having on his own family, yet also felt guilty for possibly being a "bad son" and losing his father's love if his father were to be declared incompetent and placed in a rest home.

Once he experienced the Loved Ones meditation, he was touched by how many loved ones he sensed sending him love, including his father. He stopped feeling so terribly unlovable. He was then introduced to the EFT protocol to deal with his anxiety that was overwhelming. He focused on the angst..."I will be a bad son if I have my father declared incompetent" as he did the 8 point tapping protocol. His initial anxiety level was ranked as a "9" and with one round of tapping it dropped down to a "3". After a second round of EFT, his level of distress dropped to a "1". He was amazed that he immediately felt stronger and calm and couldn't see why he had been so heavily stressed about an issue that was obviously in his father's best interest to pursue.

We discussed a regular routine of meditation and tapping to reinforce his newly calm demeanor. He was very pleased. He continues to use both meditation and his EFT protocols whenever he feels overwhelmed as he continues to cope with his father's health situation or work-related stress.

Example 3: Kate presented to my office as a new patient with ongoing conflict with her husband of 17 years. She felt that she was not being appreciated or respected in the relationship. She reported having the shadow thought that she was "unworthy" of having an unconditionally loving partner in her life that stemmed from her perception of relationships in her family of origin. This belief was causing her to experience frequent stomachaches and headaches.

She felt that she had to earn love from her husband by "doing for him" constantly. The initial level of distress for this thought was ranked at an "8". After going through the EFT protocol twice, the distress ranking went down to a 0. She then tested at a 10 for the affirming statement of "I deserve to be loved unconditionally" and "I do not have to buy/earn love". She was able to picture changing how she would behave with her husband and envision herself asking for as much respect as she was giving her husband. She was able then to understand and visualize how this was reasonable in a mutually loving relationship.

Of note, she had both gastrointestinal distress and a headache at the beginning of the office visit, but she reported no distress physically from either issue by the end of the session. She felt very happy and calm when she left my office.

KEY 2. The Obstacle of Guilt and Shame:

The experience of intimate human connection in a perfect setting is exquisite and joyful rather than painful. Relationships take many forms, among them acquaintances, families, business connections, friendships, marriage, and partners (people working toward a common goal). Often we base the dynamics of our present relationships on our past experience. For instance, if your parents were each divorced and remarried by the time you were a teenager, you may have developed a distrust of lasting relationships. You might now find yourself in relationships where you fear intimacy, rejection and abandonment. If, on the other hand, you grew up in an abusive situation, you might find yourself repetitively drawn to relationships that involve an imbalance of power and control because this feels familiar. Relationships essentially reflect the quality of the life that we create. If we were spiders, they would be the web that we weave. How beautiful is the web you are weaving in your life at present?

What are relationships about anyway? We tend to want to have one that is successful, but how do you define success? A successful relationship is not necessarily one that is meant to last forever. It could be one in which you learn forgiveness or one in which you learn self-love, or learn how to let go and walk away. Relationships are for our mutual learning and spiritual evolution whether we enter them consciously or subconsciously. Many people feel that a relationship is an exchange or an implied agreement to meet one another's needs, whether those needs be safety (take care of me, protect me), power/control, financial advantage, cultural, dependency (co-dependency, dependency or inter-dependency), common goals, or to make one feel lovable, whole, and complete.

What should we expect out of a relationship? What are realistic expectations? It is important to be mindful that we are not stagnant beings. Our journey in life and in our relationships is to grow and develop emotionally, intellectually and spiritually as individuals in the most balanced way possible. A healthy relationship is one in which both partners are supportive of fostering mutual respect and interdependence. Interdependence does not necessarily mean being obligated to meet all their partner's needs and thus negate their partner's ability to grow as a person in their own right. It means with love and compassion that you assist one another with developing one's full potential so that each person becomes whole and complete within himself or herself. In this manner, neither partner becomes excessively needy, expecting the other to meet their needs, wants and desires on a continual basis; instead, each partner is there equally compromising and sharing responsibilities, gifts and abilities. This necessitates both partners giving and taking on both sides with compassion on a daily basis.

Since we aren't stagnant beings, we are constantly changing our thoughts, feelings and circumstances, including our relationships. We may think that there is something wrong when there is a challenge in a relationship. However, what we may really need to know is what we expect from that other person in the relationship. What are the thoughts and feelings that attracted us to one another or helped to create the circumstances of our meeting? What are we meant to know and learn from one another? Sometimes an issue will arise to make us aware of how we need to grow or of how limited we are in some aspect of our relationship. How are we using each other as mirrors to reflect our potential lessons? Sometimes when we feel the other person in a relationship is being judgmental, we are actually the ones being judgmental...or angry...or jealous... or selfish...or needy...or unfair...or untrustworthy...or depressed, etc. Do you recognize any of these patterns in any relationship in your life where you are experiencing some discord? We all have done this at some time or other in our lives.

Perhaps, once we discover the answers to these questions, then we can acquire the skills and wisdom to move forward to develop relationships with a deeper level of trust, cooperation and synergy.

Challenges and tests arise when one partner shifts their behavior or dynamics in a relationship and the other partner resists. What can you do when you find yourself in such a situation? Keep yourself centered in your heart and not your guilt, shame, fear, anger and resentment. Maintain a loving energetic connection by staying as compassionate, open and understanding as possible for yourself as well as the other person. Remember that the only person you can change in any relationship is yourself. If you can continue to love and have compassion without getting angry or hurt, feeling like a victim, or guilty, or in your other negative reactive selves, then you have truly mastered the test and challenge in front of you. When you can ask for forgiveness (coming from a position of strength) for not being perfect or whatever it is that you have labeled your self to be, you can still attract positive energy into the relationship either for growing to a deeper level of connection or for lovingly letting go and moving forward. Sometimes it is appropriate to lovingly walk away from a relationship where one partner is repetitively abusive to another whether it is emotionally, physically, sexually or energetically.

During a relationship crisis, avoid going into the "poor me/feel sorry for me" mode, the reaction of guilt, shame, fear and anger, and sending out negative vibes. Remember that your wellbeing (emotional or otherwise) is not dependent on someone else's behavior. When in a state of stress, we often go into a "fight or flight" state where our bodies override our logical minds, negative patterns get triggered and we automatically react from our unconscious childhood faulty thoughts such as "I am unlovable", "You can't trust anyone", "Everyone will disappoint me or leave me, it's just a matter of time". This can wreak havoc in any relationship. Triggers from our subconscious negative scripts create judgment of self and others. When we start focusing constantly on "how is this person going to let me down", we shift into sending out negative energy while looking for the negative attributes in others.

The power to heal any relationship issue (to either move forward in the relationship or to let go and lovingly move on) is forgiveness of self and others, which really means giving up your reactive judgment of self and others. Guilt tethers you to the past and causes you to recreate negative scenarios in your life. Sometimes we have to transform the anger or shame surrounding a past event or situation before we feel fully ready to forgive our self or others. If this is the case for your situation, Key 4 – The Obstacle of Anger and Resentment may be required for you before you can truly release your self from your past guilt or sense of shame. The processes, meditations and techniques described in the 12 Keys of this book will assist you in transforming the negative core beliefs that limit you from becoming aware of all that you can be as the beautiful, energetic, spiritual being that you are, expressing all of your unique gifts and abilities in this physical realm, and experiencing the flow of joy in your daily life.

Exercises to Release You From Guilt and Shame:

1. Transforming Guilt/Shame Meditation:
Hint-This meditation will be more effective if you have a friend read it with feeling to you or you record yourself reading it with heart on an audio tape and play it back to follow as you meditate in a quiet private space. This meditation can also be found on a companion CD that accompanies this book (for details see *www.12keystoshift.com*).

Take a deep breath. As you exhale begin to let go of any tension and negativity within you. Take two more slow, deep breaths and as you exhale feel yourself being filled with light as the negativity is released.

See, sense and feel yourself walking at sunrise on a sandy path in a lush desert setting. You had no idea that a desert could be so beautiful. Notice the fluttering butterflies attracted to the beautiful colors of the flowers on the cacti as they bloom in the springtime air. Listen to the song of the various birds that live in this lush, deserted paradise. Feel the vibrations, color and sounds of love in the air flowing to you as you walk on this beautiful path in the desert.

Now look to your right and see an abandoned desolate area that looks like it was once an oasis. As you look more closely you see a few, old weathered cocoons, each attached to a decaying cactus barely growing in the dry sand. While you examine this scene more closely, one of the cocoons in particular attracts your attention.

As you curiously observe this one cocoon, it begins to slowly change into the shape of someone in your life that you have hurt, deliberately or unintentionally. Notice them standing there in the dry weathered sand. Look into their eyes and sense their bewilderment. Look even deeper into their eyes and you can sense the extent of their sorrow.

Remember the loving vibration of all the fluttering butterflies, beautiful flowers on the cacti, and the songs of the birds flowing towards you. Feel the intensity of all that love and all of your love flowing towards this one cocoon that looks so dejected and perplexed. Tell this person that you deeply regret that you caused them pain and ask that they forgive you. Feel your love going over to them as gentle as a soft desert breeze surrounding them and transforming their sorrow. (Pause) As you watch, they begin to change into a beautiful butterfly.

Feel your profound desire to lift the sadness from everyone in our world. As you set your heartfelt intention to do this, the most beautiful pink healing light begins to flow outward from your heart. Carefully observe as this pink light flows outward from your heart and spreads over the entire abandoned oasis covering and touching everything and everyone.

Notice as the other cocoons begin to transform into brilliant butterflies. Beautiful butterflies of every kind begin to flutter and alight everywhere. Feel your love flowing towards them all. (Pause) Feel your spirit soaring. Know the ability of your loving power to transform sadness into joy. It is such a delight to experience the joyous flight of all the radiant butterflies. When you are ready, feel yourself slowly returning until you feel yourself fully present in your body and gently open your eyes.

2. Loving Benefactor Meditation:
Find a comfortable, seated position on a chair or cushion and allow your body to settle into position. Close your eyes and begin to focus your attention on your breath, following your cycles of inhalation and

exhalation. Notice the rising and falling sensations on your belly as you breathe in and out and follow this for a few cycles.

Now try to bring to mind a heartfelt sense or visual image of someone whom you believe embodies the qualities of unconditional love and compassion. This person may be a friend or relative, a religious or historical figure, a spiritual being or just someone who embodies these qualities to you. Picture this person as if they were sitting or standing right in front of you.

Look into their eyes and feel the absolute unconditional love and compassion flowing from them towards you. Now radiate feelings of love and gratitude back towards this person. Once you feel the love flowing steadily between your heart and your Loving Benefactor, allow your Loving Benefactor to move to your left side until they are standing just behind your left shoulder. Now see, sense or feel someone that you have relationship difficulties with as if they were standing right in front of you. Look into their eyes and sense their confusion. Now look even deeper into their eyes and sense their sadness.

Understand how the separation between you and this person has created sadness for you both. Allow your love and the love from your Loving Benefactor to flow over toward this person who is standing in front of you. Tell this person that you love them and that you are sorry that you hurt them. Ask that they forgive you for whatever has transpired in your relationship. Tell them that you forgive them as well.

Whenever you feel your mind wandering or feel yourself becoming less loving, gently bring your attention back to the image of the Loving Benefactor and once again practice radiating love, empathy and compassion towards them. Feel their love, empathy and compassion radiating back towards you. Once you feel the connection again with your Loving Benefactor, return your attention to the person with whom you are having relationship difficulties. Allow your love and the love from your Loving Benefactor to flow towards them once more.

Feel the difficulties between you dissolving and being replaced with a feeling of peace and oneness between you. Know that relationship difficulties are always a result of a sense of separation and can be healed with love, understanding and compassion.

3. Sending Empathy Towards Oneself:
Repeat the meditation exercise above but this time picture yourself as the person with whom you are having relationship difficulties. Heal the sense of separation within you and feel a renewed sense of self-love and peace.

4. Confront Your Biggest Fears in a Relationship Exercise:
Make a list of your biggest fears in a relationship. Include the worst things that friends, family members, co-workers or others could say about you. Once you have compiled your list, do a round of EFT tapping for each fear, starting with the ones that resonate most powerfully within you or bring up the strongest emotion. Once you have completed the tapping exercises for each of your fears, you may find it helpful to repeat the above sending empathy toward yourself exercise.

5. 2nd/Spleen Chakra Exercise:
When we have shame or guilt over a situation, we are either busy judging ourselves (2nd chakra issue) or we are fearful of others judging us for our actions/inaction (3rd chakra issue). The act of forgiving our self cannot fully be accomplished until we first acknowledge that the situation exists/existed, realize that our perception that creates guilt or shame does/did not truly reflect who we really are... and then make a choice to transform our perception of the incident and deal with the situation differently.

The second or spleen chakra is located below the navel, one hand width above the pubic bone. The spleen chakra is where we hold our creative energies, our inner child and how we feel about our self. The 2nd chakra is believed to resonate with the color orange, the tone "ooh", and the musical notes of either D or G (you must discern which note is right for you).

Get into a comfortable position either sitting or lying down. Close your eyes, take a few slow deep breaths, and begin to focus on the spleen chakra. Now recall the most wondrous orange colored sunset that you have ever seen or experienced. Sense or feel the warmth of the magnificent orange colors of the sunset surrounding your body. Take a deep breath and begin to breathe into your body the revitalizing light of the beautiful orange colors. Feel the vibrant colors traveling within your body toward the spleen chakra. Continue to breathe in this wondrous light until you sense that your second chakra is fully restored with this swirling brilliant orange light. Begin to tone out loud "ooh" seven times and feel the vibration of the tone within the spleen chakra. Sense an inner peace of self-acceptance and new vitality. When you are ready, gently open your eyes.

6. 3rd and Solar Plexus Chakra Exercise:

The 3rd chakra is located one hand's width above the second chakra. This chakra is where we hold what we think about our self as well as what we want others to think about us. It is also about power and control. The 3rd chakra resonates with the color of bright yellow, the tone of "oh", and the musical note of either E or A (whichever resonates most strongly with you).

The Solar Plexus proper is actually not the 3rd chakra although it is often noted as being one and the same. In fact, the Solar Plexus chakra resides in the fleshy area just below the bottom of the breastbone (where one would perform the Heimlich maneuver). This chakra is where we experience either our fear or our fearlessness. The Solar Plexus chakra resonates with the color of olive green (the color of the uniforms of most armies throughout time), the tone "Rah", and the musical note of either F or A (use your discretion at to which one is more appropriate for you).

Get comfortable, close your eyes, take a few slow deep breaths, and focus on your third chakra. Sense or feel the presence of a powerful and brilliant golden sun before you. Feel the intense warmth of the golden rays emanating from this radiant source toward your third chakra. Notice how the energy flowing into you allows you to let go of any negativity in your mind and your judgment, allowing you to connect with who you really are. Feel the warmth and grace of this radiant sun permeating the essence of your being and filling the third chakra with the golden light of abundance and the palace of possibilities. Hold onto this sensation as you tone "oh" seven times and feel the intensity of the vibration throughout your third chakra. Now call upon the Archangel Jophiel who is the archangel of awakening wisdom, illumination, introspection, self-awareness, inspiration, hope and joy. Sense this beautiful, powerful being walking toward you from the golden light. Ask him to assist you and become aware of him placing an olive green peridot gemstone into your Solar Plexus. As this healing stone enters your body, sense the emotional healing taking place that allows you to begin to see the past or present situations causing distress more as an observer rather than from an attached emotional level. Now you can move past the hurt, anger and bitterness and find a deeper understanding in your relationships. Take a deep breath and sense the olive green color of the peridot filling your solar plexus, emanating a peaceful sense of clarity and wellbeing. Tone "rah" seven times and feel the vibration of this vowel sound resonate throughout your solar plexus. When you are ready, gently open your eyes.

7. Energy Medicine Techniques:

1.Think about a few incidents which cause you to feel guilty or a sense of shame, whether present or past. This usually works better if you focus on only one person or incident at a time. (This might be something you did or did not do, said or did not say, or something that was done to you.)

Rate your guilt or shame on a scale from 0 (none) to 10 (most) before your tapping session so that you can note improvements.

Note: This treatment will not make you immune to having guilty feelings when appropriate, but should reduce any inappropriate, self-sabotaging guilty feelings you are currently attempting to alleviate.

2.Treat the possibility of reversal by repeating one (or any that strongly resonate with you) of the below phrases three times with feeling while tapping on the KC point (if you want to be more specific for your situation, then by all means modify them):

"Even though I feel so guilty/shameful about what I did (or what was done to me), I choose to forgive and accept myself right now."

"Even though I have been harboring this guilt/shame in my mind and body and punishing myself for this incident (be specific), I deeply and completely love and accept myself and all my feelings."

"Even though I have been feeling this guilt/shame about (person's name or event), I have decided to forgive and accept myself and move on.".

3. Then tap on the following points seven times while thinking about the guilt or shame issue: EB, SE, UE, UN, Ch, CB, UA, and TH.

Then go to IF (inside tip of index finger next to the nail on the thumb side) and tap while repeating one or more of the following phrases:

"I choose to release this guilt/shame about this incident with (fill in blank)."

"I will forgive myself for this incident (fill in blank)."

"I will let go of this guilt/shame and stop punishing myself now for this incident"; or

"I feel it in my heart to forgive myself, etc" (tailor this phrase as appropriate).

4. Once again rate your guilt/shame on a 0 to 10 scale. If there is no significant decrease in the rating, go back to step 2 and do 3 more rounds of tapping with feeling. Be sure you are emotionally tuned in to the problem. You may utilize the 9 Gamut Procedure/ sandwich technique if you continue to have difficulty diminishing the feeling of guilt or shame.

5. In the event you still have no results, look for another self-sabotaging belief, reword step two with the new phrase and do 3 more rounds of tapping.

6. As long as your level of guilt/shame continues to decrease, keep tapping until there is little or no guilt or shame left. If the treatment still stalls, try tapping on your KC point and say three times with feeling: "Even though I still have some of these guilty/shameful feelings, I deeply and completely love and accept myself with all my feelings" and do some more rounds of tapping. Repeat as necessary.

7. You may choose to do the 9 gamut or the short cut procedure as described below if you still have problems reducing your guilt or shame level down to a 1 or a 0.

In the 9 Gamut Procedure, you must first locate the gamut point on the back of either hand, 1/2 inch beyond the knuckles (toward the wrist), and in line with the midpoint between the pinky finger and the ring finger. While constantly tapping the gamut point, do the following nine actions:

1. Close eyes.
2. Open eyes.
3. While holding the head still, shift eyes to lower left.
4. While holding head still, move eyes to lower right.
5. Roll eyes clockwise 360 degrees while keeping head still.
6. Roll eyes counter-clockwise 360 degrees while holding head still.
7. Hum a few bars of your favorite tune for a few seconds (e.g., "Somewhere Over the Rainbow", "Happy Birthday," "Row, Row Your Boat.")
8. Count to five.
9. Hum once again.

OR try the short version by tapping on your gamut spot while holding your head straight and moving only your eyes down to the floor and then up toward the ceiling.

As you repeat these treatments over time, the guilt or shame should go away.

6. Applying Key 2:

Example 1: As a psychiatrist I have found the Loving Benefactor meditation helpful to do before dealing with difficult patients or with patients who are in intense pain as it expands my heart and allows love and compassion to flow through me out into the room. Patients have often commented that they recall feeling tremendous compassion palpably in my office when they recount the past difficult moments of their therapy. I often will picture spiritual beings that embody compassion to me (Christ, Buddha, Kwan Yin or Mother Mary), and I can feel the energy of these beings often in the room when a patient is in a great deal of emotional pain. It is quite powerful and I can have intense sweetness, joy and love fill me when I do this. My heart truly expands when I go through this exercise. I feel more present and in the moment when I do this. I have also done this before dealing with difficult people in my personal life that I have a need to be around in social or other situations. It really has been helpful to change how I react toward them and at times has changed how they react toward me.

When I began to do the meditation exercise about sending empathy toward myself, I immediately was taken back to a meditation that I did a few years ago in which Elijah came to me. It was so intimate and powerful and caused me to have much more empathy for myself than I believe I ever have had in my life. I felt such overwhelming love coming to me and also from me to myself.

I recall an experience using the Loving Benefactor with a 6-year-old boy with severe Post-Traumatic Stress Disorder who responded incredibly well to low dose medication and some energy medicine (EFT) techniques. He had grown up in a drug house where he had witnessed horrendous violence and sexual behaviors. He was removed from this situation by child protective services and was brought to me for evaluation of his symptoms of severe anxiety, depression, flashbacks, nightmares, severe headaches and periods of dissociation where he would stare off into the distance for up to 5 minutes at a time.

My compassion went out so strongly to this brave young boy. I was amazed at how motivated he was to feel better and how he learned the techniques so rapidly. He was thrilled to have a powerful tool that put him in charge of the bad memories. At his second visit to my office, he ran up to me in the waiting room and threw his arms around me to say thank you. All of his symptoms had dramatically improved and he reported doing the energy medicine exercises any time that he had "bad thoughts" about things that had happened in the past. I felt such overwhelming compassion for this young child and yet sensed it also flowing from the Loving Benefactor toward myself. A year later he continues to blossom in his new nurturing life and he still uses the EFT techniques to deal with stress or anxiety. It is times like that that I know that I am indeed living my purpose here.

The empathy exercise toward a neutral person is a fairly easy one to do since we do not tend to have significant counter-transference reactions or strong feelings toward a neutral patient. It is a mild warm feeling and they seem to respond readily to the sense of positive energy—it tends to be an energizing experience for both of us. I had an experience recently at an amusement park (yes, I was either brave enough or stupid enough to take my 3 children—ages 12, 10 and 8—to an amusement park on a holiday weekend... chuckle). We were in line in ninety-two degree heat for a ride and a little bit ahead of us was a 30ish-year-old African American woman and her approximately 11-year-old daughter.

Suddenly the young girl began to swoon and slowly collapsed to the ground. The appalling thing was that no one did anything but just look and pretend to not see it. I ran up to her and lifted her upper body off of the cement as her mother helplessly looked on in a stunned fashion. I do not know if everyone was afraid to either get involved or to lose his or her place in line. Such a feeling of sadness for the situation and then a great love and compassion for this young girl that I had never met before filled me. I yelled for someone to give me some water (lots of folks with water bottles around since it was a hot day).... and only one single person reluctantly handed one over. I gave the girl some water to drink and then asked her mother if I could pour some over her head, as she was incredibly hot and dehydrated. As I poured the water over her head and caressed her face, I asked if she thought she could stand with her arm wrapped around my waist with her mother supporting her other side. We moved her out of line and toward a shady area; the look of absolute shock on her father's face as he saw a Caucasian woman nearly carrying his young daughter toward him where he was awaiting them in the shade will stay in my mind for a while. They both thanked me and I just was amazed at how shocked people are today at a simple act of compassion. We saw them later in the park and this young girl and her sister were lively and enjoying themselves a great deal.

It can be more difficult, but even more powerful, to use the compassion and empathy exercise with a difficult patient. I had a gentleman named Barney that I worked with for over 12 years. At many times I wondered just how helpful I was to Barney. He had a history of severe childhood trauma and perceived himself to be a black hole for negativity. He often said that he believed his purpose in this life was to absorb all the negativity and abuse so that no one else would have to suffer from it. Sometimes it seemed that the best thing I could do for Barney was to remain as a non-judgmental, compassionate presence for him.

Although I felt inadequate at times in therapy with him, I also knew that just being there and being fully present for him as he worked on whatever he could tolerate working on at the time had kept him from being hospitalized or even from killing himself. He had had numerous hospital stays and suicide attempts before we started the therapeutic journey together. I had to remind myself many times that I can only assist someone with healing at their time and pace.... not the time and pace that I would wish for them. It was a great lesson in tolerance and compassion... and that is the gift in it I suppose.

Barney passed away during the time that I was working on this manuscript. His death was sudden; a heart attack on a warm, spring morning. He was 63 years old. I again wondered how much I had really done for him or assisted him in his healing journey. Just when I was questioning once more what I might have done differently, Barney's wife contacted me. She sent me a card with a long letter and a copy of Barney's obituary. She wanted me to know how grateful the family was for the years of care and compassion shown to Barney, and how much it had meant to Barney that I had stood by him in his journey without giving up on him.

Example 2: I have worked with setting intentions for the past several years and have seen a big change in my daily experiences, especially as I have done it increasingly mindfully. I taught a powerful lesson in consciously setting intentions a few years ago with my sister whose husband had undergone a liver transplant. She was angry and frustrated with the attending physician who would not stop during clinical rounds at her husband's bedside to answer her questions. She felt she had a right to have her questions answered as she herself had been the one to donate 2/3 of her own liver to her husband, and she had been involved intimately in his care at her husband's request. She had gotten to the point that she always felt angry and guilty that perhaps she had somehow done something to displease the doctor as the doctor and his entourage of residents breezed through the room and completely ignored her.

While I was at the hospital in Manhattan with her, it was time for the doctor to make their clinical rounds. The nurse announced that the attending had just gotten to the floor and would be coming in shortly. I could feel my sister tense up immediately and "felt" her resentment (as well as her husband's) and sense of shame permeate the room. I told her to sit calmly and talked her through a meditation of feeling her tension and resentment release with each slow, deep breath. Then I had her picture her own heart filling with love for her husband (and for the 2/3 of her own liver which now resided in her husband's body); and I asked her to feel her heart expanding out to fill the entire room. I told her to send her love out and to surround this attending physician also with love and Light. Then I instructed her to just sit quietly in the windowsill of the room and to not say a word, but just to send love out as the whole team of doctors entered the room to make their rounds.

She was at first uncertain of doing this, stating "He won't stop to let me ask questions; he never does". I just replied to her, "If you do this, he WILL today". Both she and her husband thought I was too optimistic but she stated she would at least try it since nothing else had worked. So we just sat in the windowsill, said nothing, and just sent love out to the whole team as they came to "look at the wound" and to check the labs.

When they stopped their clinical banter, they turned and started to leave the room; but then suddenly, as the attending physician had almost walked out of the room and had his back to us, he turned around with a perplexed look on his face. He then smiled and started to talk to us. He asked if we had any questions. He then stood there and answered a number of questions calmly and completely for about 8 minutes (apparently a record for his surgical demeanor as one of the transplant nurses later came back to tell us that they couldn't recall when he had ever spent so much time with answering questions - he usually sent a resident back in to do such a thing).

My sister finally "got it" that day and always set her loving intention during visits after that day. She saw a complete change in demeanor from herself toward her husband's doctor as well as from the doctor towards her.

Key 3. The Obstacle of Abandonment

Many of us get stuck when we feel alone or have a sense that we have been abandoned by friends, partners, family or often ultimately by the Divine. What else can cause the perception of abandonment? We often feel abandoned when a relationship ends or shifts, when we are a child and a sibling is born, when we feel that we have failed in some fashion, when we get sick and our perception of our self has changed, when we feel that we have been abused or punished or humiliated, when we feel disconnected, when we relocate, when we travel and do not have our support system around us, when we are in a relationship of codependency and our partner is no longer meeting our expectations, or when we are in fear of change.

When we feel abandoned, we often neglect to request assistance from others. Why? We may feel embarrassed or fear that we will appear weak if we ask for help. We may feel unworthy of assistance. We may feel that others need help more than we do so we feel guilty for asking for help for our selves. We may feel too vulnerable or too stoic to ask for help because we may fear rejection. We feel that no one cares about our life.

At the moment that we perceive ourselves to be abandoned, we generally shut everyone else out; and we isolate our self even more. We come to believe that we must only rely on our self to deal with stressors or life circumstances. Our ego may keep us from asking for help as it walls itself off from experiencing further pain. But we can ask for Divine

Assistance discreetly without any one else being aware that we have done so.

What is Divine Assistance? For that matter, what is the Divine? The Divine refers to powers or forces that are universal or transcend human capacities. All faith belief systems throughout time refer to some type of divinity or divine beings that offer assistance to humans ranging from angels, archangels, cherubim, djinn, elementals such as dragons in Chinese traditions, salamanders and sylphs in Celtic tradition, tree and river spirits from Roman mythology, Muses and Fates from the ancient Greeks, and animal beings from Native American and Australian aboriginal tribes. Each faith also espouses certain avatars or enlightened beings that have come to assist humans at various times in history such as Christ, Buddha, Mohammed, Quan Yin, Lao Tsu to name a few. Ancient Mystery traditions teach that that every human is in essence a part of the Divine manifesting in the physical world.

Believe it or not, IF such a thing as Divine Assistance exists, then why would we have to ask? What do we have to lose? Suspend your judgment and entertain the following for a moment. What if there IS a Supreme Being as many theologies profess? What if that Supreme Being truly started out as the only thing existing in a void? Imagine being that Supreme Being and deciding what you might create. How about starting with Light since in the beginning there is nothing but darkness? So you send out "the Word" or a vibration of creation and.... voila.... there is Light. Well, that is good. Now the Supreme Being might just sit in that for a few eons to experience every aspect of Light versus Darkness. However, once every aspect of that is experienced, then he/she might want to try creating in a different way. Well, then perhaps the next step would be to take an aspect of one's own self and reflect it out in front of you... suddenly you have archangels and angels that are impulsed by the will of the Divine or Supreme Being. However, those archangels and angelic beings are creating directly from the impulse of the Divine will to assist with creation as they have no will of their own... so that might get a bit boring after a while too. Eventually, this Supreme Being might come up with an interesting notion or Divine Plan.

How about taking an aspect of his or her own self and flinging it out so far from him or her that it forgets that it is OF the Divine? What would this aspect of the Divine create if it did not know where it had come from? Now this interesting Divine experiment could only work if this aspect of the Divine were granted its OWN free will to create in whatever manner it chose and was not impulsed solely from the Supreme Being's will. How about flinging this divine being out into the physical realm and how about creating a veil that would make it difficult initially for that divine being to recall where it had come from? Now it gets really interesting from a creation viewpoint!

How can the Supreme Being experience EVERY possible aspect of creation? Send all these beautiful beings out into the physical and get them all creating at once! See what they will create with each choice they make! Now that IS cool, eh? Okay, don't get upset… we said just ENTERTAIN this thought for a moment. We don't want to step on anyone's beliefs or dogma. Wouldn't that be an exciting experiment?

So why do we pray? Certain theologies have told us to "Ask and ye shall receive" and "Knock and the door shall be opened". More recently, authors espousing the popular ancient concept of the "Law of Attraction" have suggested that we need to put the vibes out there to have the universe respond in kind; just as we ask the genie from the lamp, we put in an order from the catalog of possibilities from the universe to deliver to us our wishes. It is possible to have your wishes responded to if they are your true genuine desires (this will be discussed further in Key 11), just as it is possible to request assistance in your daily life as you face tests and challenges in your journey through this lifetime. We essentially pray in order to request assistance as well as to express gratitude to a spiritual/universal being or power.

The common denominator here is that we must each learn to speak up and ask—express our needs, wants and desires. This is important in our daily lives in order to get what we want or need from family, friends, co-workers and others. If we don't ask for something or let someone know what we want or need, how do we expect to receive it? We are not by and large a society of mind readers.… So SPEAK UP! After all, we do not drive up to our favorite fast food restaurant and tell them when they ask what we want to order: "Well… I don't want the burger…and I don't want the fries…. I don't want the chicken…. I don't want the shake…" Imagine how frustrating it is for both of us, the one not speaking up about what they really want and the person attempting to assist us!

Below you will find a series of exercises that can help shift whatever may be preventing you from feeling connected, speaking up, or asking for assistance from others.

Exercises for When You Feel Alone or Are in Need of Assistance:

1. Assistance Meditation:
Hint- This meditation will be more effective if you have a friend read it with feeling to you or you record yourself reading it with heart on an audio tape and play it back to follow as you meditate in a quiet private space. This meditation can also be found on a companion CD that accompanies this book (for details see *www.12keystoshift.com*).

Close your eyes, take a deep breath and, as you exhale, feel any stress and tension washing away. Take another deep breath and as you exhale feel yourself relaxing even more. Sense yourself walking on a path up a gently sloping hillside leading to an ancient and beautiful forest.

Ahead in the distance, just inside the perimeter of the forest, you can see the edge of a small stream with shimmering light reflecting off the surface of the clear, cool water. As you near the bank of the river, you drink in the beauty of the lush, green plants and the refreshing earthy scent of nature surrounding you.

The splendor of iridescent blue and green dragonflies dancing along the glistening water catches your eye and you are drawn to follow them along the water's edge, and deeper into the ancient woods. There is a sense of familiarity as you experience the energy of this sacred place deep inside the forest.

You suddenly become aware of a large opening in the hillside, on the opposite side of the river. You increase the pace of your stride, as your anticipation grows stronger. You carefully follow a series of nine stepping-stones to carry you safely across the river to the secret and up until now hidden opening in the hillside.

As you cross the threshold of the entrance to the immense cave, you are struck with awe as you become aware of beautiful, gleaming crystals lining the walls of the cavern. You follow a very old worn path leading to a brilliant shaft of light coming down from above in front of a wall of streaming water.

You are amazed that the intensity of this pure light causes you no discomfort. Stepping into the light, you are drawn to the center where an ancient rock formation creates a natural, comfortable place to rest. From the vantage point of nature's throne, you are able to further appreciate the play of light sparking on the surface of the gently cascading water flowing down the surface of the gleaming stone wall.

It is as if the water cleanses your mind and energy as it flows and carries away all negativity, resistance and stress. You feel the powerful and soothing energy of the light shining down on you in this secret sacred place that is your own personal sanctuary in nature.

As you look up into the radiant light that streams in above you, you become aware of a sensation of warmth; and a gentle, almost tingling, sensation on your face, top of your head and in your hands. While you curiously observe this light more closely, you realize that there are beautiful, loving, spiritual beings within this light; and they are sending love to you.

Feel the pure love flowing to you from these beings of light that are there to assist and support you. Tell these beautiful, angelic beings that you acknowledge them, and are ready to allow them into your life. As you state this, the light gently pulsates and the brilliant crystals lining the walls of the cavern begin to emanate light to you.

Each crystal with its own color and unique vibration, represents the divine strength and assistance that is available to you for any situation, need or purpose. This assistance is available to you at any moment; all you need do is ask and it will be given.

Feel the joy these beings of light have for you making the connection with them. Feel the joy in your own heart as you realize that you are never alone; no matter what is facing you in your daily experience.

Know that your sanctuary will always be there for you. You now know the way.

Spend as much time as you like in your special sanctuary. When you feel you are ready to return to your physical world, feel your self slowly returning to your body. When you feel your self fully present, gently open your eyes.

2. Thymus/High Heart Chakra Exercise:

Although most of us are used to doing for others in the world (at work, at home and in our communities), there are many of us who have difficulty with allowing our self to receive from others. True abundance entails being able to both give and receive. If we do nothing but give our energy out to others, we will rapidly become depleted of energy ourselves; and then we may become sad or resentful because others "took" our energy that we freely gave.

The High Heart chakra is the only chakra that is paired and is not located in the center of the body. It is located between the 4th and 5th chakras on either side of the center of the body at the level of the thymus, approximately 3 inches above each nipple. This chakra is about balancing our male energy (yang/physical/doing) on the right side with our female energy (yin/spiritual/receiving) on the left side. Whenever there is an imbalance in the High Heart Chakra, there is an issue involving lack of self-nurturance/allowing oneself to receive (left side) or fear of doing/taking action (right side) in your life. This chakra is energetically tied to the thymus gland in the body; and an imbalance in this energy center may cause immune dysfunction in the physical body. The thymus chakra resonates with the color turquoise, the tone "yah", and the musical note F#.

Get into a comfortable position either sitting or lying down. Take a deep breath and as you exhale, feel your muscles relax. Take 3 more slow, deep breaths and feel your muscles relaxing even more. Focus on your High Heart Chakra. Become aware of each of these energetic centers on either side of your body. Sense where there may be less or more energy -- visualize it as if there is one delicate golden scale with two balancing plates, one residing in each of the small, paired chakras. Now picture a basket of exquisite turquoise stones etched with ancient yet familiar symbols standing before you. You find yourself attracted to certain stones, as their symbols appear to have great meaning for you. You find it easy to choose the appropriate number of turquoise stones that create a perfect equilibrium when placed on either side of the scale. Note the symbol on each stone that you have chosen and feel the message it brings to your heart. Feel a greater sense of vitality as the scale becomes balanced. When you feel yourself perfectly balanced, take a deep breath and, as you exhale, gently open your eyes.

3. 5th/Throat Chakra Exercise:

The throat chakra is located one hand's width above the heart chakra at the neck area of the body. The 5th chakra is believed to resonate with the color blue, the tone "I" or "eye", and the musical note of either G or C (you must discern which note is right for you). The throat chakra is where we hold the energy of our creative expression. There is often a block in the energy of the throat chakra when someone is afraid to express themselves freely either out of fear of being judged by what they say (either by self or others), fear of not being heard, or fear of hurting someone else by what they express. A block can also be caused by constantly expressing out of anger, resentment or frustration. The following exercise will assist with releasing such blocks.

Get into a comfortable position either sitting or lying down. Take a deep breath and feel your body relaxing as you exhale. Take two more slow, deep breaths; and, as you exhale, feel yourself relaxing even more. Now see, sense or feel yourself walking outside on the most beautifully clear starry night. It is amazing how bright all the stars are and how clearly you can see each one. As you continue to walk, you become aware of what looks like a bright blue shooting star that appears to have landed on the ground in the distance. You begin to approach the area and realize that you see the glowing light of a campfire up ahead. As you draw nearer, you see a group of people gathered around the fire. They appear to be dressed in garments from various times and places; and they smile and encourage you with heartfelt eyes to join them -- as if they have been waiting there for you for a very long time.

As you look around the circle, you sense a connectedness to these people. It feels as if you have known them forever. One of the group members with whom you feel particularly connected approaches and embraces you; they reveal that they have been waiting for you to ask for assistance and know that you are now ready to receive whatever it is that you need to fully express whom you really are in the physical world. They further convey that their whole purpose for existing is to assist you at this very moment.

It is time for your voice to be energized so that you may express yourself more clearly, from a place of joy rather than fear or anger in your life. The entire group begins to chant "I" and it feels only natural to begin chanting out loud along with them. The song of your voice joins in with the others and continues for several moments. You curiously observe the one who is leading the initiation, reaching into the blue flames of the fire; and painlessly pulling out the most brilliant blue sapphire you have ever seen. The leader smiles at you with love as he or she gently places the sapphire into the area of your throat chakra. You feel a gentle, vibrant, loving energy expanding outward from the brilliant sapphire and surrounding your body. You feel any negativity being released from your throat. You sing out "I" more clearly and powerfully than you have ever expressed before, with joy and gratitude. The leader smiles at you with light-filled eyes that say, "I will always be here for you".

When you feel that you are ready, feel yourself slowly returning to your body until you are fully present; and gently open your eyes.

4. Energy Medicine Techniques:
1. Think about those times when you have either felt lonely, abandoned, or unworthy of help in any form; or think of a time when it felt like there was no assistance, divine or otherwise, available for you. On a scale from 0 (none) to 10 (most) evaluate the level of distress the following statements provoke before your tapping session so that you can note improvements.

"Even though I feel so lonely (or… fill in the blank… abandoned, all alone, disconnected, etc.) and I feel there is no one or nothing there to assist me, I deeply and completely love and accept myself with all my feelings."

"Even though I am not sure I want to reconnect with God (or Supreme Being, Universe, Higher Power, etc) because he/she let me down (add any feeling that pertains to you), I completely love and accept myself anyway."

"Even though I don't feel safe reconnecting because (fill in the blank), I completely love and accept myself and all my feelings anyway."

"Even though I don't believe in divine assistance, I completely love and accept myself with all of my feelings."

"Even though I feel left behind and am angry at God (or Supreme Being, Universe, Higher Power, etc), I choose to reconnect now."

"Even though I feel so undeserving of any assistance spiritual or otherwise, I deeply love and accept myself with all my feelings."

"Even though I don't deserve help and if I ask for it, I won't get it anyway (I won't be heard), I deeply and completely love and accept myself with all my feelings."

"Even though I am afraid to ask for assistance, because I will be taking assistance away from someone who needs it more that I do, I choose to love and accept myself with all my feelings; and I will ask for help anyway."

"Even though I am afraid that, if I ask for assistance, I will be judged by what I ask for, I deeply and completely love and accept myself and choose to ask anyway."

2. Treat the possibility of reversal by repeating one (or any that strongly resonate with you) of the above phrases three times with feeling while tapping on the KC point.

3. Then tap on the following points seven times while thinking about the issue that resonates with you: EB, SE, UE, UN, Ch, CB, UA, and TH.

4. Once again rate your feeling on a 0 to 10 scale. If there is no significant decrease in the rating, go back to step 2 and do 3 more rounds of tapping with feeling. Be sure you are emotionally tuned in

to the problem. You may utilize the 9 Gamut Procedure/ sandwich technique if you continue to have difficulty diminishing the intensity of your issue.

5. In the event you still have no results, look for another self-sabotaging belief, reword step two with the new phrase and do 3 more rounds of tapping.

6. As long as your level of distress continues to decrease, keep tapping until there is little or none left. If the treatment still stalls, try tapping on your KC point and say three times with feeling: "Even though I still have some of these feelings or beliefs, I deeply and completely love and accept myself" and do some more rounds of tapping. Repeat as necessary.

7. You may choose to do the 9 gamut or the short cut procedure as described below if you still have problems reducing your guilt, shame, unworthiness or sense of disconnection from God/Source/Spirit level down to a 1 or a 0.

In the 9 Gamut Procedure, you must first locate the gamut point on the back of either hand, 1/2 inch beyond the knuckles (toward the wrist), and in line with the midpoint between the pinky finger and the ring finger. While constantly tapping the gamut point, do the following nine actions:

1. Close eyes.
2. Open eyes.
3. While holding the head still, shift eyes to lower left.
4. While holding head still, move eyes to lower right.
5. Roll eyes clockwise 360 degrees while keeping head still.
6. Roll eyes counter-clockwise 360 degrees while holding head still.
7. Hum a few bars of your favorite tune for a few seconds (e.g., "Somewhere Over the Rainbow[2], "Happy Birthday," "Row, Row Your Boat.")
8. Count to five.
9. Hum once again.

OR try the short version by tapping on your gamut spot while holding your head straight and moving only your eyes down to the floor and then up toward the ceiling.

As you repeat these treatments over time, the negative feeling or shadow thought should go away.

5. Applying Key 3:

Example 1: Terry is a 40-year-old married female who had been healthy her whole life. She presented to me with acute anxiety after she discovered during a routine mammogram that she had several small calcifications in her left breast (a potential sign for malignant cancer). There were no similar findings in the right breast. They were read as "inconclusive" by 2 different radiologists and her gynecologist felt that to biopsy each of the areas would be so disfiguring that removing the breast might be a better option. He left the decision up to Terry to either wait 3 months to repeat the mammogram or to biopsy one or two of the areas. She opted to wait and her gynecologist agreed that it was a reasonable decision.

Stressed and frightened, she began to examine her life and her own self-nurturance issues. She was a pediatrician and had spent much of her life focusing solely on the needs of others rather than her own needs (her patients, her children and her husband). She was spiritual and was accustomed to requesting spiritual assistance for helping others but had never requested it for herself. She never felt worthy enough to speak up about her own needs or desires and ask for assistance for herself; she felt that would be selfish.

After 3 weeks of therapy, she began to change her perceptions and started to create more of an energetic balance in her life -- respecting her self and nurturing herself as much as she did others. She set firmer boundaries in her relationships and created time for her self-care. Terry began meditating and requesting divine assistance for herself daily. She began to feel a greater sense of inner peace and purpose. She truly developed her voice to speak up more in her life in a loving manner. She no longer felt like a victim in her life and she took charge and responsibility for creating the type of life she desired to live.

At the follow up mammogram, the radiologists and gynecologist were astonished that the findings showed nothing but healthy breast tissue.

Example 2: Lynn is a 35-year-old married female who presented initially with anxiety due to job-related stress and some marital tension. She felt overwhelmed at times with her responsibilities both at the office as well as at home. She described herself as spiritual but felt some difficulty attending church due to issues with church dogma. She felt more in her head and less connected with God over the years.

We discussed the importance of reestablishing a spiritual connection for her since she described feeling empty inside and had little internal direction. She was interested in reconnecting and feeling the way she had felt as a child -- joyful, open, free and connected. She felt completely alone in the world despite having a husband, family and friends. This was an all-too-familiar complaint among the patients in my practice.

After she experienced the above Assistance Meditation, she wrote me the following note: "The area I go to for spiritual assistance is cleansing and empowering. It is where I breathe best. The Light is powerful, and I feel warmth in this light. It also feels preparatory, a place to concentrate on the journey within. This is the place to meet with Michael the archangel and the other angels. If I am resistant to looking inward, this is the place where I can shed my resistance. I have been picked up and carried by angels upon request after I have asked for assistance. The angels are often chattering and anxious to get going and assist me.... As if they are extremely excited to help. The column of light that I see seems to transport angels and other golden-orbed beings down to my inner temple. There is much energy in the light-it has also been the site of conflict, where Archangel Michael will say to me 'Help me to push away this darkness'. My spiritual sanctuary is readily available and if necessary a place I can get to in a hurry. Its time takes on a very different characteristic. It loses its association with Earth time." Her anxiety resolved once she felt her connectedness once again and she no longer felt alone. She knows now that spiritual assistance is always available upon request.

Example 3: Chris is a 30-year-old female who presented originally with anxiety over stress in her marriage after her husband lost his job following an injury. She was a devout Christian and attended church regularly yet felt a sense of disconnection. While she routinely prayed for others on a daily basis, she felt a sense of unworthiness regarding requesting direct spiritual assistance for her self. She attended our weekend intensive meditation course and began to understand the concepts that are presented in this book. Two months after taking the course, she continued to use the tools described in this book on a daily basis.

One day while she was leaving her mother's home to drive to a nearby store, she was involved in a terrible car accident. Members of the fire department had to cut her out of the car with the "jaws of life" and were concerned that she would lose the use of her legs, as the whole front end of the car was crushed when she was hit head-on by an 18-wheeler truck hauling logs. She later reported that when she turned the curve and saw the truck heading directly for her in her lane, she knew that she could not prevent the collision.

Chris immediately used a tool that she had learned in the 12 Key course to prepare her self for the crash. She thought of the symbol she had received in a meditation that represented a request for immediate spiritual assistance to achieve the unachievable. Her mother was one of the first people to arrive at the scene, driven by her own intuition that something was very wrong. Chris was the one who reassured both her mother and the EMS attendants that she was going to be okay; and that she had asked for God and angels to protect her and assist with instantly healing her body. She reported that she could wiggle her toes and that she KNEW that she was okay. EMS attendants thought she was in shock and delirious. She instructed her mother to "contact Tracy and Marion" to do long distance healing on her as EMS was putting her into the ambulance.

Chris was bruised, yet walking on her own, within a week. Her doctors were amazed at her rapid recovery. She continues to use her tools daily and no longer suffers from anxiety.

KEY 4. The Obstacle of Anger and Resentment

What causes our feelings of anger and resentment towards others and our selves? When we feel that we have been wronged, violated, or abused, or when we feel disappointment, hurt, or trauma, we often become angry about the event and the people whom we feel caused the negative situation. We also can become angry or resentful because we felt humiliated, manipulated, betrayed, judged, not valued or validated, or because we felt just plain ignored and not heard. We may experience anger when we feel out of control, when we feel others are trying to control us, when we feel stupid, or when we disappoint ourselves because we expect our self to be perfect. It may be caused by something as simple as making a mistake or failing.

We may experience chronic states of anger at times; in fact, much of the world seems to be in a chronic state of anger at the moment, with the press and politicians fueling the response. What if you consider the possibility that we are reflections mirroring the world? What if the world situation is actually mirroring what is going on internally within the collective consciousness of us all?

There are indeed legitimate reasons to feel angry (violation of one's rights as a person or acts of broken trust), but more often than not we become angry in response to feeling out of control, believing we are helpless, or feeling like we are a victim of other people, events or life circumstances. Rather than blame everyone else for our anger, we need to take responsibility for our feelings and accept and deal with the problem or situation at hand. Nobody actually makes us angry.

We choose to be angry due to our interpretation about what other people's actions mean about us. Whenever we choose to harbor anger and resentment toward someone else or even toward our own self, then we actually tether our self energetically to that person or situation and continue to draw to us similar negative experiences. Energy follows thought. We tend to energize or draw to us that which we dwell on or think about repetitively.

Forgiveness is a harsh idea to accept as a response to anger, especially toward someone whom you feel has hurt you. Forgiveness is not about condoning the other person's actions or about not recognizing that you were wronged. The boss who fired you without cause, your cheating spouse, the rapist, burglar, or person who mistreated you was still wrong in their actions. In forgiveness there is actually clarity in discernment between the action and the person. You do not have to like them or say that what they did was okay in order to forgive them.

The bottom line is that when we choose to be angry we are the ones who suffer the physical, psychological, emotional and spiritual consequences of these feelings, not the ones at whom we are angered. If we hold on to this anger, we may become physically or emotionally ill. Medical studies have shown that heart attacks and strokes have been linked to holding on to anger. Some chronic pain conditions, such as fibromyalgia and rheumatoid arthritis, are also worsened when we harbor anger and resentment. In addition, depression can, in some cases, be caused by anger turned inward toward our own selves. Our state of anger can become chronic; and then what kind of energy in the form of persons and situations are we going to attract?

Have you ever known someone who constantly had a black cloud of negativity and chaos following them around in their life? We all have known someone like that; in fact, we have all been someone like that at some point. Take the following example of Gus: Gus was new to the neighborhood. When he first met his next-door neighbors, he asked to borrow their lawnmower because his had just broken and his grass was 6 inches high in his yard. He apologized profusely for the imposition but explained to them: "Nothing good ever happens to me." Gus was in chronic ill health and stated that he seemed to be breaking down just like his tools and equipment. The neighbors reassured him that he was just having a run of bad luck and that things would likely get better now that he was making a move and a new beginning for himself.

A week later, the neighbors met Gus in his driveway to inquire what had happened since his right leg was in a cast and he was on crutches. Gus gloomily stated: "I told you nothing good ever happens to me… I fell down the stairs and broke my leg." He was once again reassured that his luck would surely change soon. Six months later, on a chance meeting, Gus informed the neighbors that his wife had left him for another man and that he had been fired from his job because "nothing good ever happens to me". At the next neighborhood mixer, a new family had moved to the community and Gus' neighbor remarked to them, "Watch out for Gus; he has a black cloud following him everywhere he goes…. Nothing good ever happens to him!"

In the above example, Gus constantly sees himself as a victim of the world. He doesn't realize that he is very powerful in assisting with creating his own circumstances with his own angry and resentful thoughts, feelings and expectations. He is not yet enlightened to the concept that he manifests his own reality much as one would draw back a mighty bow and place an arrow in it to shoot out into the world, to powerfully draw to him that which he sends out.

The Bow and Arrow Theory of manifestation is as follows. The bow represents our emotional intention (i.e., anger, resentment, fear, love, compassion). The strength of the emotional intention determines how powerfully we draw back our bow to send our thoughts out into the world to manifest. For instance, if there is not much power behind the emotion, then the arrow will scarcely fly. If, on the other hand, there is great power behind the emotion (such as rage), then the arrow will fly quickly and can create rapidly and profoundly in our lives. The arrow represents our thought, which directs the intention. The thought will direct how the intention (or great emotion) will actually manifest in our life. It is important to note that we cannot create for anyone else. We can only draw back our own bow to create in our own life. If we draw our bow back with the intention of harming others, we will only draw similar negative energy into our own lives.

Now, back to the example of Gus. Gus is just like the rest of us; he too draws back his bow most powerfully with the emotion of intense anger or resentment, anxiety or fear, and great love or compassion. With a powerful intention, his thoughts will manifest very rapidly in his life. With a weak emotion or intention, the arrow will scarcely fly as the energy will rapidly disperse and will have minimal effect on his life. Thus, Gus has created for himself intensely in the above scenario with great resentment over his perceived "poor me" life predicament. Gus, like all of us, can only create for himself and, as he sends negativity out into the world, he manifests more negativity and chaos in his own life.

Below is a diagram of how Gus draws his bow back with anger and resentment to manifest powerfully in his life. Gus essentially pulls back his bow with the intention of anger and the arrow he loads it with is the thought "All I ever get is crap!" What he creates is crap. He has no great love or passion in his life; and, while he does not have a dog in his life, a dog did leave a little gift for Gus on his "path".

Now see what the diagram might have looked like if Gus had chosen to transform his anger and resentment and draw his bow back with nothing but compassion for himself and for what was his most heartfelt desire to create in his life. It is a completely different awareness and reality of life. The arrow he now chooses to place in his bow is the thought "I wish to have more love and abundance in every form in my life". Once again, energy follows the power of your intent (emotions); and the way that energy is directed, or manifests in your life, is dependent on your thoughts. Gus now creates love in his life in the form of a dog and a companion as well as financial abundance.

Forgiveness is about choosing to release and let go of past negative experiences, such as anger and resentment; and enabling our self to move on in our lives with an attraction of healthier positive energy, people and situations. You are very powerful in your choices and how you choose to draw back you own bow. Do you want to draw your bow back with anger and resentment in your life? Or will you choose to transform those negative thoughts and emotions so that you may consciously draw your bow back with compassion and love to manifest what is your most heartfelt desire in your life? You are, in fact, a powerful energetic being manifesting daily in your physical life. It is always within your power to make the choice to stay stuck or to shift.

Exercises for Transforming Anger and Allowing Forgiveness:

1. Transforming Anger and Resentment Meditation:
Hint- This meditation will be more effective if you have a friend read it with feeling to you or you record yourself reading it with heart on an audio tape and play it back to follow as you meditate in a quiet private space. This meditation can also be found on a companion CD that accompanies this book (for details see www.12keystoshift.com).

Close your eyes. Take a deep breath and as you exhale, feel yourself beginning to relax. Take two more slow, deep breaths and as you exhale, feel yourself relaxing more and more.

Find yourself walking on a secluded path at dusk in the countryside. The firmness of the ground under your feet keeps you fully present. In the distance you see a rising mound of earth that you are slowly approaching. There seems to be something present at the top of the mound rising before you.

As you near the summit, you become aware of a circle of stones in the center of which is nested a tall clay vessel. You curiously observe the urn more closely and become aware of something smoldering within it. You can see the hint of smoke curling over the brim against the twilight sky.

As you stand before this pot, begin to become aware of all the anger or negativity that is simmering within you; this anger may be past or present from your childhood, adolescence, or adulthood. Be aware of both the personal anger from your daily frustrations as well as the universal anger linked to world events and situations.

Feel this anger and resentment gathering and releasing from around your heart as a black cord and traveling over to this clay urn. As the anger, resentment and negativity enters the earthen vessel, observe the shift of wisps of smoke into actual flames of fire that reach into the darkening evening sky.

As more of the feelings of anger and resentment fan and fuel the fire, there begins to be a transformation of this negative energy. The fire extends into the sky and transforms into threads of beautiful light pulsating into the air as an aurora borealis of whirling energy, dancing in the night sky. Feel the anger and negativity releasing and altering, being replaced by a sense of freedom and joy, as it becomes a wondrous, shimmering, healing light.

Continue to stand there and release any residual negative feelings until you sense that they have all been completely transformed. It feels so good to let go of all that anger.

Take a deep breath and sense how you can breath easier and more fully when you are not so confined by the cords of negativity. You feel lighter and freer than you have ever felt before. Feel the peace. Now look up at the incredible night sky full of twinkling stars and brilliant planets, knowing that you have your part in creating all this beauty as you transform your anger into healing love.

When you feel ready to return from your journey, feel your self slowly returning to your body, fully present, and gently open your eyes.

2. Energy Medicine Techniques:

A. EFT Technique for Transforming Anger:

1. Think about an incident or person, whether in the present or past, that has caused you to be angry. This usually works better if you focus on tapping to deal with one person or incident at a time. Rate your anger on a scale from 0 (none) to 10 (rage) at the beginning of each tapping session so that you can note improvements.

2. Treat the possibility of reversal by repeating one (or any that strongly resonate with you) of the following phrases three times with feeling while tapping on the KC point (if you want to be more specific for your situation, then by all means modify them; phrases you don't use now you can use in subsequent rounds):

"Even though I feel so angry about what happened, I deeply and completely love and accept myself with all my feelings."

"Even though I feel so angry at (name) …I can forgive them as they did not know any better at the time and I deeply love and accept myself with all my feelings."

"Even though I am punishing myself by remaining angry for this incident or with this person (be specific), I deeply and completely love and accept myself and all my feelings."

"Even though it doesn't feel safe to let go of this anger, I choose to let it go and choose to love and accept myself with all these angry feelings."

"Even though it doesn't feel right to forgive this person (fill in the name) for what they did, I deeply and completely accept and love myself anyway with all my feelings."

"Even though I am so angry at (name) for what happened, I am ready to forgive them because they were doing the best they could at their level of consciousness – and the best they could do really wasn't good enough – and I deeply and completely love and accept myself anyway with all my feelings."

Then tap on the following points seven times while thinking about anger or any of the above affirming phrases: EB, SE, UE, UN, Ch, CB, UA., and TH

Then go to (LF) little finger (inside tip of pinkie fingernail on the thumb side) and tap while repeating one or more of the following phrases:

"I choose to release myself from this anger."

"I will forgive myself and (fill in blank for person, place or event) as I know he/she/it did not know any better or were doing the best they could do at their level of consciousness."

"I choose to let go of this anger and stop punishing myself now for this incident. "

"I feel it in my heart to forgive myself, as I am doing the best I can do, etc". Tailor this phrase as appropriate.

4. Once again rate your anger on a 1-10 scale; and, if there is no significant decrease in your ranking, go back to step 2 and do 3 more rounds of tapping with feeling. Be sure you are emotionally tuned in to the problem.

5. In the event you still have no results, look for another self-sabotaging belief, reword step two with the new phrase and do 3 more rounds of tapping.

6. As long as your level of anger continues to decrease, keep tapping until there is little or no anger left. If the treatment still stalls, try tapping on your karate chop point and say three times with feeling: "Even though I still have some of these angry feelings, I deeply love and accept myself" and do some more rounds of tapping as necessary.

7. When your level of distress drops to 2 or less, then do the 9 gamut or the short cut as described below.

In the 9 Gamut Procedure, you must first locate the gamut point on the back of either hand, 1/2 inch beyond the knuckles (toward the wrist), and in line with the midpoint between the pinky finger and the ring finger. While constantly tapping the gamut point, do the following nine actions:

1. Close eyes.
2. Open eyes.
3. While holding the head still, shift eyes to lower left.
4. While holding head still, move eyes to lower right.
5. Roll eyes clockwise 360 degrees while keeping head still.
6. Roll eyes counter-clockwise 360 degrees while holding head still.
7. Hum a few bars of your favorite tune for a few seconds (e.g., "Somewhere Over the Rainbow", "Happy Birthday," "Row, Row Your Boat.")
8. Count to five.
9. Hum once again.

OR try the short version by tapping on your gamut spot while holding your head straight, while moving your eyes down to the floor and then gently look up at the ceiling, while at the same time you deliberately project your vision and old energy out into the distance.

If your level of distress is not down to 1 or 0, go through the entire tapping sequence once again.

As you repeat these treatments over time the anger should diminish.

B. Chi Gong Exercise for Releasing Anger:

Think of an issue that makes you feel angry. Stand with your feet shoulder width apart and your hands at your sides. Tuck in your pelvis and slightly bend your knees, as if you were sitting on an imaginary tall stool behind you. As you breathe in, slowly bring your hands up at your sides to the level of your shoulders with your arms straight and as you reach the height of your shoulders, turn your palms upward facing the sky. Then continue to raise your arms, bringing your hands over your head. Make a fist with each hand. While making a loud "Tchu" or "Chew" sound, forcefully exhale while rapidly bringing down your arms all the way to thigh level and opening your fists, flinging and releasing the angry energy into the earth. Feel the tension releasing from your muscles as you perform this maneuver. Repeat this motion at least 3 more times or until you feel the anger completely released.

3. Ceremonial Anger Release:
Write down on a piece of paper the issue that is creating anger or resentment for you. This may be in a form of a letter to the person with whom you have the issue or may just be your own angry thoughts that you are feeling. We present three ways of performing this ceremonial release. You may, of course, create your own ceremony that feels appropriate for you.

The first ceremony involves tying your note to a helium balloon and releasing the note into the air to be carried away. (Note: Make certain that you have no identifying information on the note that you have written if you choose to use this method as the balloon will inevitably pop once it reaches a high altitude and your note may return to the earth several miles away.)

The second ritual involves burying your note in the ground to allow the anger to be released and transformed by the earth.

The third way of transforming anger is performed by burning your note outside in a ceremonial fire or in a fireplace. Of course, be sure to contain your ceremonial fire in a safe manner; never leave a fire untended, and make certain you have water, sand, or a fire extinguisher to put the fire out when you are finished with your ceremony.

4. The 'La Cucaracha' Technique:
If you have to be around a person that you harbor anger towards and you are not yet ready to transform the anger or resentment, then this technique may be helpful to you. Picture the person as a giant cockroach. While this may sound bizarre, it can really work. Think about it. A cockroach is completely predictable; it will come out in the dark and runs to hide when the light is on. We do not expect the cockroach to act any differently on any given day. The level of consciousness of a cockroach dictates that it will indeed come out in

the dark and run to hide when a light is on. We do not get angry at a cockroach for not coming out when the lights are on.

Think about someone who repeatedly annoys you. If you really think about it, aren't their behaviors pretty predictable after a while? The specifics may change but the pattern probably remains fairly stable over time. Isn't that person sort of like a cockroach; or, for those of you squeamish about cockroaches, like an ant in one of those plastic ant farms you might have had as a kid? Remember how those ants would move the piece of bread around while you were away at school, or out playing, or while you slept at night? Yet you didn't sit there and scream at the ant or beat on the side of the fragile plastic walls of the ant farm, did you? If you did, this exercise may not work for you.

Now, think of the person whom you are harboring anger towards and see them as if they are a giant ant or cockroach wearing human clothes, with their antennae bobbing around on the top of their head and their little insect arms dangling off their sides. If you picture this image when you are around the person in question, then you will likely not be so attached to their behaviors and will not take what they say or do so seriously or so personally. Sometimes it can help to hum softly under your breath, "La cucaracha, La cucaracha....". The Spanish term for cockroach is "cucaracha".

You will have more of a sense of humor towards the person angering you, your self, and the situation in general if you use this technique. Of course, you should remove your self from any abusive situation. This would not be an appropriate means of dealing with someone who is physically, sexually or emotionally abusive towards you.

Applying Key 4:
Example 1: Lila is a 55-year-old female who presented with powerful anger directed toward both her father and brother. In her Southern family dynamics, women were not valued as much as men since only men could pass on the family name. Although she had worked diligently and whole-heartedly full-time in the family run business and assisted with making it extremely successful in her community, upon her father's death the entire business and family assets were left to her brother who had participated minimally in the business.

Lila had repeated dreams of stabbing her brother to death. Feeling consumed by her anger, Lila was unable to move forward in her life. She became depressed and suicidal due to her anger that was also directed at herself, for devoting such time and energy to her family over the years and having her loyalty repaid in such a fashion. Her father died of a chronic illness; Lila had sold her home and moved in with her father to help care for him as his health declined. She felt she was a loving and devoted daughter. Her brother, on the other hand, was not close to either parent, had done little to care for his father except in token manners, and had lavishly spent much of the family funds on himself and his family during his father's illness.

Antidepressants assisted with decreasing the intensity of the crying spells and the suicidal thoughts, yet Lila felt little passion for living, had a low energy level and little motivation. She isolated herself from her remaining family and friends and became very reclusive. She spent much of her time in bed or in physical pain as she reported that her whole body ached. Sleep was the only effective means she found to numb herself from her anger.

After suffering for several months, she was finally ready to take some responsibility for transforming her anger rather than wait for me or a medication to do it for her. She used the tools in Key 4 to begin to tackle her anger a piece at a time (anger at her father for betraying her, anger at herself for allowing it to happen, anger at her brother for spending the family fortune and for being responsible for the line of succession). The brother also terminated Lila's position and health insurance once he took over the family business and after their mother also died for whom Lila had been primary caregiver.

Lila diligently meditates several times a week now and uses the EFT tapping techniques on each aspect of her anger. She has found renewed energy, purpose and enthusiasm in her life. While she has taken a few steps forward and a few steps backward over time, Lila overall has made progress. She feels more empowered and less of a victim of her family and social circumstance. Issues remain but they are increasingly in the background as she works on her further healing and begins to move forward in her life. She is beginning to create a program in her community to help developmentally disabled children. She states she feels it is her purpose in life at present, which is a huge step for her.

Example 2: Peter is a 72-year-old male who is an ex-minister of a Christian faith. He presented with severe depression and suicidal thoughts. Feeling disconnected from his professed faith, God, his family and his second wife, Peter was overwhelmed by guilt and shame. He had removed himself from any position in the church as he felt unworthy, describing himself as a "drunk and a womanizer". Peter's suicidal thoughts dissipated with the use of an appropriate antidepressant medication. However, he had found minimal benefit from standard psychotherapy approaches and still felt quite depressed.

Before we had met him, Peter had been in therapy for several years for depression and his feelings of anger, guilt and shame. He had been actively involved in Alcoholics Anonymous and had been abstinent from alcohol after being diagnosed and treated for esophageal cancer 3 years prior. After meeting with him for two sessions, it was apparent that Peter's primary issue was one of self-hatred. He was angry with himself for being weak, setting a bad example for his congregation and family, his inability to resist temptation, and going against every teaching he had professed.

Peter felt drawn toward an alternative approach to his issues and he was desperate to change. He knew he could not live much longer in such intense emotional pain. He met with both Marion and Tracy separately several times and began to pursue the teachings that we cover within the 12 Keys. After he began to use the 12 Keys techniques regularly, Peter began to experience compassion for him self, and that enabled him to open up his heart even more to others. His heart had previously been shut down due to his intense anger.

Peter felt a renewed connection to God and a love for himself as a spiritual being. As he renewed his creative expression in art and music; he became active in pursuing his passion for sculpting. He took a sculpting class and his first major piece was featured in a major regional student art show. His life has taken on a new direction and he is once again active as a leader in his church. He has begun to truly live again.

Key 5: The Obstacle of How We Define Our Self

The true and fundamental essence of each and every person is actually peaceful and loving. In today's Western society, however, our sense of peace has become disturbed and distorted due to our attachments, misperceptions, and faulty beliefs, all honed through our life's experiences. We have gone from being heart-centered to being fear-centered. The peace we once experienced has shifted into anger, love has transformed into fear, and happiness has evolved into confusion and sadness.

Our ego is trained and shaped by our society, media, parents, teachers, educational institutions, religious figures and culture in general to identify with everything that we are not; such as our professions, roles we play in our lives (spouse, parent, child), nationality, religious dogma, or political belief systems. There is a perception of reality that has been created for us. Increasingly over time we actually see this reality to be true and accept it as our own. This creates an experience of separation, lack, and futility, as we perceive our selves to be in competition for limited resources of love, wealth, power, control and happiness. It appears that there just isn't enough for all of us. Rather than defining our selves as connected to everyone else, we perceive our selves to be isolated and disconnected except through externally imposed social groups. We even actively search for differences to separate our selves further, dividing us into groups of nationalities, religions, race and ideologies.

We have become a society in which we avoid looking within to see who we really are. We have seemingly perfected the art of distraction. Where there was once a place in our heart as young children where we lived in wonderment and a sense of connection to everything and everyone, we now live in a perpetual state of distraction with the advent of technology such as computers, the internet, television, movies, video games, and telephones. Rarely does anyone ever sit in stillness. When we do stop for a rest, we seem to have to be constantly entertained or numbed to our emotions. There seems to be no room for introspection, bird songs, nature, and being still enough to get in touch with one's own true essence.

We spend the first half of our life looking into our outer space and forgetting about our inner space. Then we spend the second half of our life trying to find life's deeper meaning and eventually look into our inner space to find out who we really are. How do we reach the turning point and decide to begin to look within? Often it takes a crisis in our life to cause our attachments to be abruptly wrenched from our grasp and strip our ego and force us to look within. For others, the quest begins with a sense of emptiness and lack of fulfillment, even when we believe that we have achieved all of our goals as set forth by us or by the standards of our society.

When we have lost touch with our true essence, we are not fully present in our daily lives. Think back to yesterday. Where was your attention? What did you focus on? Was it on problems and duties? Were you fully present or were you focused on the past and/or the future? Recall yesterday. Did you feel peaceful? Calm? Centered? Did you have a sense of clarity? Did you feel a sense of power without a need to be in control? How much time did you spend in your thoughts? How much time did you spend in your feelings? How much time did you spend in your heart? Did you flow through your day with a sense that you were empowered and that you empowered others?

The point of all these questions is that, if you did not experience your day from a standpoint of empowerment and joy, you likely were not fully present and in the moment at that time. You were not in touch with your true essence. You were being all too human, struggling between thoughts and emotions, ideas and feelings, failure and success;

you were essentially caught up in some aspect of ego. The problem with living life from the standpoint of our ego is that there is never any resolution, never enough, only more struggle. That place from which our peace and power and joy come from is called our true self or true essence. That is the self that we have to invoke, call in, touch, understand and become reacquainted with so that we can let that all-knowing part of us flow into the lives that we have created.

Contemplation and meditation is a necessary step in transformation, whether personal or social. How do we step out of our ego, shift our consciousness away from everyone else's beliefs, and find out which beliefs or knowings are truly ours? Contemplation is one of the most effective ways to let go of attachments that distort our sense of self. Meditation assists with gaining insight into eternal truths and removing the blocks that prevent us from experiencing the inner peace of our true essence. Mindfulness meditation assists us with relaxing the mind and entering an internal space where we enable our selves to stand as an observer to our thoughts and emotions, allowing them to float by freely as if clouds passing in the sky to which we do not become attached. However, contemplative/meditative practices, whether sitting still or moving as in tai chi or walking meditation, must be on-going and disciplined in order to remain connected to our inner peace as the external world can readily ensnare each of us in the chaos and fear-mongering in our daily lives, as described by the media and politicians of our time.

Exercises for Reacquainting Your Self with your True Essence:

1. Mindfulness Meditation:
Mindfulness allows us to see the arbitrary, conditioned nature of our thoughts that prevents us from becoming aware of whom we really are. It assists us with cultivating compassion for ourselves as we connect with our personal perception of suffering and transcend it, as we realize that it is a temporary condition with a beginning, middle and an end. Mindfulness meditation also helps us increase compassion for others when we also become aware that everyone has their own suffering in their life. No one person's suffering is more or less than another; it is relative and one person's pain is as legitimate as another's.

Mindfulness meditation can help to develop global empathy when we sense or feel that we are more than just individuals alone here on the planet and realize that we are all connected to one another, feeling our part in the universe and our interconnectedness. Mindfulness exercises can give us insights into the chains of our own thought processes that we bind ourselves or limit ourselves with. Once we become aware of those thoughts and realize how faulty they are, it leads us to freedom because we can shift our thoughts as we realize how beautiful and powerful each of us really is. Mindfulness meditation helps us see the big picture where we can identify with something greater than ourselves like nature, friends, family, community, religious figures, spiritual teachers, etc.

'WHO AM I?' Mindfulness Meditation:

The objective of this meditation is to watch the mind's answer to this question at as many levels as possible, as we ask this question several times. We seek to better understand how the self or ego is constructed by our thoughts and makes us feel separated from the essence of who we really are. Try this exercise alone or with a friend or partner. If you try it alone, it can be even more powerful sometimes if you do this exercise in a comfortable sitting position as you look into a mirror in low light, looking deeply into your own eyes each time you ask the question: "Who am I?" If you are doing this exercise with a partner, sit facing one another, looking deeply into one another's eyes, and decide who asks the question first: "Who are you?" After the person responds just keep asking repetitively: "Who are you?" "Yes, I know you are that, but who are you really?" Each time the answer is taken to a deeper level. Switch roles after 15 minutes.

After the above meditation ask yourself the following questions and consider journaling your answers:

How do I perceive myself? How do others perceive me?

Think about how your life would be different if you were not so concerned about your image or how others viewed you and you were lead by your inner knowing and intuition.

Did this exercise bring up labels (mother, father, lawyer, etc)? Have you asked yourself the question: "Is this how I really define myself? Sometimes? All the time?" Are you also inclined to see the bigger picture and see yourself as connected to others or the "whole" as a part of the universe?

Did your awareness go to self-concerns and self-judgments? Can you consider that self-judgments are only thoughts? Did this meditation lead to feelings of anger, frustration, pride, pain or other negative emotions? Did you notice how the intensity of each emotion has a beginning, middle and an end and that the period of our suffering has a limit to it?

2. True Essence Meditation:

Hint-This meditation will be more effective if you have a friend read it with feeling to you or you record yourself reading it with heart on an audio tape and play it back to follow as you meditate in a quiet private space. This meditation can also be found on a companion CD that accompanies this book (for details see www.12keystoshift.com).

Close your eyes and take three slow, deep breaths. With each breath, breathe in gold and white light and feel that light entering into your lungs, traveling into your bloodstream and from there journeying to every cell, atom and molecule in your body. As you exhale, feel yourself releasing any negativity that is within you until eventually you are completely filled with light and exhaling light out into the room. Sense the room filling with light.

See or sense yourself standing outdoors in a peaceful place that you know well. Feel the warmth of the sun on your face. Immerse yourself in the sights, sounds and scents of this serene place in nature. Up ahead is a beautiful path of light. Feel yourself stepping onto this path of light and feel yourself being lifted higher and lighter, lighter and freer, freer and lighter, gently spiraling upward until you find yourself arriving at a gateway. This is the entryway to your personal paradise, the garden of your true essence.

Continue on this path of light, passing through the gate and notice a wondrous abundant garden filled with tranquility, peace and love. Be aware of all the beauty. As you continue to follow the path, it winds around a turn that you cannot yet see beyond. You wonder what is ahead.

Continue to follow the path and as you round the turn you are awed at the panoramic scene that stands before you. There is a vast and breathtaking sea extending out into the horizon. It draws you to the water's edge. Feel the healing ocean breeze as it caresses you. Breathe in the healing gentle wind and feel yourself completely relaxing.

Now call your name three times silently from the center of your heart, beckoning to your true essence to come forward. Watch as your true self appears in the distance on the beach and slowly walks towards you. Your true essence appears to you in its most enlightened human form.

Observe the feet of your true self as he or she stands before you. Notice every detail as you slowly lift your gaze upward until eventually you are looking directly into the eyes of your own true essence. Feel the beauty of your true essence and become aware of the qualities that make your true self who they are. You are gazing into your own soul, the essence of who you truly are.

Feel your true self place their hands of light upon your heart. Feel your own true essence reawakening your qualities and innate gifts that may have been long forgotten. Sense those abilities and qualities flowing into you and feel the completeness as you recognize and remember who you really are.

Look deep into the eyes of your true self and feel their absolute acceptance and unconditional love for you, exactly as you are right now. Your true self puts their arms around you and gently holds you. Feel yourself letting go completely in the arms of your true self. Now feel your true essence merge with you. Feel the oneness. Feel the power. Feel the healing that comes with the unity.

When you feel that you are ready to return to your physical world, feel yourself stepping once again onto the path of light, taking with you all of your reawakened gifts and abilities so that you may express them in your life and in the world. Place your hand on your heart and feel your love and strength, knowing that there is nothing that you cannot accomplish. When you feel yourself fully present, take a deep breath, and gently open your eyes.

3. Becoming Aware of Your True Qualities Exercise:
Take a piece of paper and print you name vertically in large block letters down the left side of the page. Write as fast as you can without thinking. Write three personal positive qualities next to each letter of your name, qualities that begin with that letter in your name. Example: Robert

R – Radiant, Relevant, Resourceful
O – Open, Original, Omnificent
B – Brave, Beloved, Beautiful
E – Excellent, Enlightened, Evolved
R – Resilient, Remarkable, Resolve
T – Terrific, Thoughtful, Trustworthy

For the next week, whenever anyone calls your name, instead of hearing your name and cringing, think of each of these wonderful attributes and qualities that describe who you really are. Keep the list in a place where you will see it daily to further remind you of how wonderful you truly are.

4. Acknowledging Joys and Blessings Exercise:
Write down ten things you have a heartfelt appreciation for in your life or ten blessings in your life.

When you acknowledge the joyous experiences in your life, you increase your awareness of all that is good and beautiful. When you become more aware of your joyous experiences and a heartfelt appreciation of them, it attracts more experiences of goodness and plenty into your life. It can also help to keep a journal of gratitude in which you record daily your joyful experiences or things for which you are grateful.

5. Energy Medicine Techniques:
Hydrate and do the 3 thumps before proceeding.

1.Think about a time when you felt so uncomfortable with your own thoughts, actions or feelings that you hardly recognized yourself and didn't want to be in your own skin. On a scale from 0 (none) to 10 (most) evaluate the level of distress the following statements provoke before your tapping session so that you can note improvements.

"Even though I feel so mean (or…fill in the blank… irritable, angry, cynical, controlling, judgmental, abusive, etc.), and I don't know how to change, I deeply and completely love and accept myself with all my feelings."

"Even though I am not sure I really am a nice person and I am afraid that people will find out that I'm not, I completely love and accept myself anyway with all my feelings."

"Even though I am too afraid to change my perception of who I am for who am I without my hat? I choose to completely love and accept myself anyway with all my feelings."

"Even though I need to wear the armor of my persona to feel safe in the world, I completely love and accept myself with all my feelings."

"Even though if I change, others will be hurt and won't know what to do; I choose to completely love and accept myself with all my feelings."

"Even though I feel helpless to change and have no control anyway, I deeply love and accept myself with all my feelings."

"Even though I am afraid of failing to change and know I am not capable of changing anyway, I deeply and completely love and accept myself with all my feelings."

2. Treat the possibility of reversal by repeating one (or any that strongly resonate with you) of the above phrases three times with feeling while tapping on the KC point (if you want to be more specific for your situation, then by all means modify them; phrases you don't use now you can use in subsequent rounds).

3. Then tap on the following points seven times while thinking about whichever statements above gave you the biggest buzz or level of distress: EB, SE, UE, UN, Ch, CB, UA, and TH.

4. Once again rate your level of distress on a 0 to 10 scale. If there is no significant decrease in the rating, go back to step 2 and do 3 more rounds of tapping with feeling. Be sure you are emotionally tuned in to the problem. You may utilize the 9 Gamut Procedure/ sandwich technique if you continue to have difficulty diminishing the intensity of your issue.

5. In the event you still have no results, look for another phrase that resonates more for you, reword step two with the new phrase and do 3 more rounds of tapping.

6. As long as your level of distress continues to decrease, keep tapping until there is little or none left. If the treatment still stalls, try tapping on your KC point and say three times with feeling: "Even though I still have some of these feelings or beliefs, I deeply and completely love and accept myself" and do some more rounds of tapping. Repeat as necessary.

7. You may choose to do the 9 gamut or the short cut procedure as described below if you still have difficulty reducing your level of distress down to a 1 or a 0.

In the 9 Gamut Procedure, you must first locate the gamut point on the back of either hand, 1/2 inch beyond the knuckles (toward the wrist), and in line with the midpoint between the pinky finger and the ring finger. While constantly tapping the gamut point, do the following nine actions:

1. Close eyes.
2. Open eyes.
3. While holding the head still, shift eyes to lower left.
4. While holding head still, move eyes to lower right.
5. Roll eyes clockwise 360 degrees while keeping head still.
6. Roll eyes counter-clockwise 360 degrees while holding head still.
7. Hum a few bars of your favorite tune for a few seconds (e.g., "Somewhere Over the Rainbow", "Happy Birthday," "Row, Row Your Boat.")
8. Count to five.
9. Hum once again.

OR try the short version by tapping on your gamut spot while holding your head straight and moving only your eyes down to the floor and then up toward the ceiling.

As you repeat these treatments over time, the negative feeling or shadow thought should go away.

Applying Key 5:

Example 1: Chet is a 70-year-old married male who presented to me for evaluation for significant depression. His depression started after he found out that his adult daughter had been sexually abused in childhood by a neighbor. He reported such intense guilt over what had happened and beat him self up continuously over how he could not have known what was going on. He had been physically and verbally abused in childhood and had thought that he had provided a good childhood experience for his only child. He truly believed that he must be a terrible person.

He decided to attend our intensive 12 Keys weekend workshop but was skeptical that he would experience any insight or relief from his depression. He pursued it merely as a last resort since both medication and therapy were only partially helpful. He felt he had no connection spiritually, and he reported a desire to "get things right with God" since he felt he only had a few years left to live. He already had severe cardiac disease and had undergone quadruple coronary artery bypass surgery. His blood pressure was under poor control; and he neglected his own self-care and recommendations to exercise due to poor self-image and the belief that he was unworthy of saving.

Chet experienced the True Essence meditation above. He came out of the meditation very tearful and reported the tears were from intense joy and gratitude. He reported: "I believe that I AM somebody for the first time in my life!"

His whole demeanor was transformed in the days and weeks that followed. He continued to use the tools that he had learned from the 12 Keys. His family was astonished by the transformation. He felt energized and began to diet and exercise. He began to pursue hobbies that brought him joy. His daughter no longer felt guilty that she had caused her father such depression and she too began to shift in her perceptions. Although they still have to cope with the effects on their family from her childhood abuse, they no longer perceive themselves as victims of the world. Chet now acknowledges his gifts, attributes and abilities as a spiritual or energetic being. For the first time in his life, he feels a true spiritual connection and a sense of being unconditionally loved.

Example 2: Wendy, a 38-year-old married female, came to see me with moderate anxiety and depression. She had problems sleeping, felt exhausted, and was overwhelmed with guilt following an extramarital affair. She had lost her motivation and passion for living.

She had been married for 15 years to a salesman who over time had become a regional manager for a large corporation, and spent most of his time on the road and little time with his family. Due to her husband's frequent absences, she was responsible for raising their 3 children, ages 3, 5 and 7, on her own. She felt lonely, confused, resentful and abandoned. She described that she felt she had lost her identity.

Before marrying and having children she enjoyed singing in small musical groups. It was her true passion and her way of creative expression. Of course, her loss of her identity didn't happen overnight. It resulted from a series of choices that led to a shift of perception. Gradually, as her husband had become more successful in his career and their family grew in size, she had less time to pursue her passion.

This story is all too familiar. How many of us have put different hats on in our lives and then identify ourselves solely with the hat we are currently wearing. Wendy felt trapped in her roles as dutiful mother and dutiful spouse. There was no balance between her needs and the needs of her family; and she made no distinction between her needs as an individual and the collective needs of the family. Her identity was completely absorbed into her dutiful roles.

In the course of her therapy she began to gain insight into her choice to look outside of her marriage and her self to find her sense of identity. She began to understand that it was fruitless to look outside of her own self to find fulfillment as it only lead to a greater sense of emptiness to seek what she was looking for through someone else. During her course of treatment she was given the tools mentioned above in Key 5, and she began to reacquaint herself with her true essence, who she was without the hats.

Wendy had forgotten how beautiful and talented a person she really was. She also became aware that everyone in the family had their own true essence and wore their own hats. With that realization she found herself more nurturing, compassionate and loving towards herself, her husband and her children. She found a better balance as she began to speak up about her needs and her husband became responsive. She had never expressed her feelings before and found that when she could finally express herself, her husband did respond. A new sense of understanding emerged in the relationship. She was able to love herself enough to pursue that which brought her great joy and started singing again in her life.

Example 3: Jack, an intelligent, single 40-year-old male, presented initially with anxiety, depression and intermittent paranoia fueled by an overwhelming fear of others. He had defined himself completely by one incident of betrayal. This occurred after he was terminated from his job as a middle level executive.

Jack was convinced that his company had used him as he had dedicated all his time and passion to his job. Whereas, he used to identify himself solely as dutiful employee; he now completely defined himself as a victim of Corporate America. He could only wear one hat at a time. We discussed medication several times and he flatly refused to consider that option, as that would mean he would have to trade his hat from being a victim to being a crazy person.

We taught Jack several of the concepts and tools described in Key 5. Jack used these tools daily over the course of eight weeks, and his anxiety and paranoia subsided. He was so excited to realize that he could regain control over his emotions and thoughts. When Jack understood that he could get into his heart and connect with his loving, true essence, he was capable of transcending anxiety and depression. He now uses these tools as his daily self-care routine.

Jack was able to recognize his own gifts and talents and how he had not been honoring them in his previous corporate position. He became aware that he had been identifying himself as someone he wasn't (his fears). As Jack reconnected with whom he really was, his passion and joy for living returned and he began to set his own course and make different choices. He chose a new career path that truly honored his gifts, talents and abilities and allowed him to express who he really was. He stepped out of his narrowly defined box in which he had imprisoned himself, and he began to blossom.

KEY 6. The Obstacle of Lack of Self-Love

Isn't it funny how many of us feel guilty whenever we do something nurturing for our self or feel like we are doing something wrong when we put ourselves first? Unfortunately, many of us were taught explicitly or implicitly during childhood that it was selfish to even think of oneself before anyone else. After all, didn't we all hear the sayings: "Do unto others as you would have others do unto you" and "You are your brother's keeper"? Perhaps a unique perspective is to recall that we are all connected; we are all spiritual, energetic beings that are connected to one another. I am a reflection of you and you, in turn, are a reflection of me. Therefore, if I decide that I will do for you and everyone else and not do anything for myself because it would be "selfish", then I am in fact choosing not to do anything for you either since I am but a reflection of you.

We seem to be held back from nurturing ourselves due to self-judgment or fear of judgment from others who would deem us selfish and, therefore, not a good person if we think of our self first or tend to our own needs. Often we are hindered from taking care of our self due to a sense of guilt or shame since we do not feel worthy of considering our own needs. Will I be loved if I take care of my own needs? Do I have to earn my love because I can't get it myself? Is it safe to do for myself? There may also be cultural or tribal norms that influence how readily we give up a sense of self or fulfill our sense of self. Some have never experienced a sense of self due to familial issues (abusive situations, a sense that their birth was an unwanted addition to the family, or a sense that the family desired a child of the opposite gender).

Consider the possibility that how we regard our selves is communicated to every cell, atom and molecule of our body. Think of every cell in your body as if it were an 18-month old toddler; because a toddler expresses all of their emotions immediately with no filtering mechanism in place, and they take to heart every word spoken to them. Recall the last time you saw a child of this age being praised for something. Do you recall the glow of joy on their face and how they almost danced? Now recall the last time you saw a child of 18 months being yelled at and told how bad or stupid or ugly they were. Do you recall the response of utter shame, sadness and the sense of their spirit withering immediately within their small body?

Now picture each cell in your own body responding to the self-talk you have running in your head daily about your own body, actions, reactions and abilities. How many times a day do we say to our self: "I am ugly", "I look awful", "I am stupid", "I am not good enough", "I can't do it alone", or "I wish I were dead"? Now imagine how the cells, atoms and molecules of your own body respond to such statements. Imagine how they might respond differently if you repetitively looked in the mirror and told yourself: "I am beautiful", "I am deserving of love and happiness", "I am capable of doing anything I set my mind to", and "I choose to fill my life with joyful and loving experiences".

Imagine the potential damage done to our cells and our selves as a result of faulty thoughts we created from past experiences. Such damage can only be reversed by embracing new, loving thoughts that counteract the old ones. It is time to develop a new loving dialogue with our selves and our cells that can only begin by awareness and then by learning and practicing self-love and self-nurturance. There is nothing selfish about regarding yourself with as much love and compassion as you have for everyone else in your life. It is a matter of balance: have as much compassion for everyone else as you have for yourself, and regard yourself as compassionately as you do everyone else.

Exercises for Self-Love and Self-Nurturance:

1. Self-Love Meditation:

Hint- This meditation will be more effective if you have a friend read it with feeling to you or you record yourself reading it with heart on an audio tape and play it back to follow as you meditate in a quiet private space. This meditation can also be found on a companion CD that accompanies this book (for details see www.12keystoshift.com).

Close your eyes. Take a deep breath breathing in love and light from the universe. Take two more slow, deep breaths filling your self completely with light and exhale light out into the room.

Imagine that you are putting on your most comfortable walking shoes. As you begin to walk down a country path, you see a trail of thousands of pink rose petals showing you the way. The fragrance of the rose petals is sweet and succulent as you walk along the path. You know these flowers were placed there just for you and with every step you feel your heart expanding more and more. Take another deep breath and feel the warmth in the center of your heart allowing the love and your worthiness of it to be accepted and felt deeply.

Look ahead and you will see the path leads to a small beautiful cottage with lovely trees all around it. This is your cottage that has been calling to you for a long time. It appears to be so inviting. Walk toward the cottage until you come to the front door. Acknowledge the color of the door as you stand there.

This is a very unique cottage. When you walk into the cottage, you will find an intimate room furnished with everything that you love and that makes you feel good. Walk in and look around. Be conscious of everything that appears in the room. Notice the various colors in the room. Sense the elements in the room that make you feel the best. Now think of everything that makes you feel exceptional and loved and as you think of it, it will appear in the room.

Now look for another door in the back of the room, opposite the front door. Scan the room until you see it. Even though the cottage seemed small from the front, it is rather deep. Walk to the door and stand there a moment. When you open the door you will find a hallway with several doors on the left and many doors on the right. One of them will lead you to a very special room.

Now open the door and go inside. Proceed down the hall and you will know intuitively which door leads to the room that is your special room. When you find it, stand in front of the door but don't go in yet. Be aware of the color of the door. This is your special room that has been awaiting you. This room contains everything related to long-denied passions, desires, pursuits and interests, everything that you never had or thought you never deserved to have.

Open the door and go inside. As you think of everything that you have denied yourself yet secretly desired, it all suddenly appears in this room. Spend as much time here as you wish and do not leave out anything that comes to your mind or to your heart. Allow yourself time to enjoy your special room.

Know that this space will always be available to you for pampering and nurturing yourself. Whenever you feel you are ready to return to your physical world, feel your self slowly returning to your body. When you feel yourself fully present, take a deep breath, and gently open your eyes.

2. Loving Benefactor Meditation:
Find a comfortable, seated position on a chair or cushion and allow your body to settle into position. Close your eyes and begin to focus your attention on your breath, following your cycles of inhalation and exhalation. Notice the rising and falling sensations on your belly as you breathe in and out and follow this for a few cycles.

Now try to bring to mind a heartfelt sense or visual image of someone whom you believe embodies the qualities of unconditional love and compassion. This person can be a friend or relative, a religious or historical figure, a spiritual being or just someone who embodies these qualities. Picture this person as if they were sitting right in front of you.

Look into their eyes and feel the absolute unconditional love and compassion flowing from them towards you. Now radiate feelings of love and gratitude back towards this person. Whenever you feel your mind wandering, gently bring your attention back to the image of the loving friend, historical person or spiritual being and once again practice radiating love, empathy and compassion towards them. Feel their love, empathy and compassion radiating back towards you.

Stay with your Loving Benefactor and feel their love flowing to you and your love flowing to them for up to 20 minutes. Know how lovable you are to this Loving Benefactor. Know that this Loving Benefactor is sending you love every minute of every day.

3. Loving Benefactor and Self-Love Meditation:
Find a comfortable, seated position on a chair or cushion and allow your body to settle into position. Close your eyes and begin to focus your attention on your breath, following your cycles of inhalation and exhalation. Notice the rising and falling sensations on your belly as you breathe in and out and follow this for a few cycles.

Now try to bring to mind a heartfelt sense or visual image of someone whom you believe embodies the qualities of unconditional love and compassion. This person can be a friend or relative, a religious or historical figure, a spiritual being or just someone who embodies these qualities. Picture this person as if they were sitting or standing right in front of you.

Look into their eyes and feel the absolute unconditional love and compassion flowing from them towards you. Now radiate feelings of love and gratitude back towards this person. Once you feel the love flowing steadily between your heart and your Loving Benefactor, now see, sense or feel yourself as a child standing right in front of you.

Look into the eyes of your inner child and sense their confusion. Now look even deeper into their eyes and sense their sadness. Understand how the separation between you and your inner child has created sadness for you both. Allow your love and the love from your Loving Benefactor to flow over toward this inner child who is standing right in front of you.

Tell your inner child that you love them and that you are sorry for any disappointment, pain or sense of abandonment that they have suffered. Ask that your inner child forgive you for whatever has transpired in your relationship. Tell them that you forgive them as well for whatever; it no longer matters what created the division between you. Recognize that it is now time to heal. Allow your love and the love from your Loving Benefactor to continue to flow to your inner child, bringing further healing. When you feel the healing is complete, hug your inner child and feel the oneness with them.

If at any point you feel your mind wandering or feel yourself becoming less loving toward your inner child, gently bring your attention back to the image of the Loving Benefactor and once again practice radiating love, empathy and compassion towards the Loving Benefactor. Feel their love, empathy and compassion radiating back towards you. Once you feel the connection again with your Loving Benefactor, return your attention once more to your inner child, allowing your love and the love from your Loving Benefactor to flow towards your inner child once more.

Feel the difficulties between you dissolving and being replaced with a sense of peace and oneness between you and your inner child. Know that relationship difficulties are always a result of a sense of separation and can be healed with intention, love, understanding and compassion.

Over time you may wish to repeat this exercise and allow your inner child to slowly mature each time you do this practice. In this manner, eventually you will be able to express and feel love for your own self in the present on a daily basis.

4. Energy Medicine Techniques:
1. Hydrate and lovingly do the 3 thumps before proceeding.

Recall a time when you felt guilty or selfish about thinking about your own needs before those of your family. On a scale from 0 (none) to 10 (most) evaluate the level of distress the following statements provoke before your tapping session so that you can note improvements.

2. Treat the possibility of reversal by repeating one (or any that strongly resonate with you) of the following phrases three times with feeling while tapping on the KC point (if you want to be more specific for

your situation, then by all means modify them; phrases you don't use now you can use in subsequent rounds):

"Even though I believe that everyone else's needs are more important than mine and they deserve to have their needs met more than me, I deeply and completely love and accept myself with all of my feelings."

"Even though I believe everyone will think I am selfish and no one will like me if I have as much compassion for myself as I do for others, I deeply and completely love and accept myself anyway with all of my feelings."

"Even though I don't believe that I am deserving of self-love because of what I did/said or didn't do/say, I deeply and completely accept myself anyway with all of my feelings."

"Even though I don't deserve to love myself because I am unlovable or such a burden on everyone else and I should be punished instead, I deeply and completely accept myself anyway with all of my feelings."

"Even though I feel so mean (or…fill in the blank… irritable, angry, cynical, controlling, judgmental, abusive, etc.), and I don't know how to change, I deeply and completely love and accept myself anyway with all of my feelings."

"Even though I am not sure I really am a nice person and I am afraid that people will find out that I'm not, I completely love and accept myself anyway with all my feelings."

"Even though I don't like myself because of what I did, what I didn't do or what was done to me, I choose to give up judgment of myself now and accept myself anyway."

"Even though I am too afraid to change my perception of who I am for then who would I be? I choose to completely love and accept myself anyway."

"Even though I need to wear the armor of my persona to feel safe in the world, I completely love and accept myself."

"Even though if I change, others will be hurt and won't know what to do, I choose to completely love and accept myself."

"Even though I feel helpless to change and have no control anyway, I deeply love and accept myself and all my feelings."

"Even though I am afraid of failing to change and know I am not capable of changing anyway, I deeply and completely love and accept myself."

"3. Then tap on the following points seven times while thinking about whichever statements above gave you the biggest buzz or level of distress: EB, SE, UE, UN, Ch, CB, UA, and TH.

4. Once again rate your feeling on a 0 to 10 scale. If there is no significant decrease in the rating, go back to step 2 and do 3 more rounds of tapping with feeling. Be sure you are emotionally tuned in to the problem. You may utilize the 9 Gamut Procedure/ sandwich technique if you continue to have difficulty diminishing the intensity of your issue.

5. In the event you still have no results, look for another phrase that resonates more for you, reword step two with the new phrase and do 3 more rounds of tapping.

6. As long as your level of distress continues to decrease, keep tapping until there is little or none left. If the treatment still stalls, try tapping on your KC point and say three times with feeling: "Even though I still have some of these feelings or beliefs, I deeply and completely love and accept myself" and do some more rounds of tapping. Repeat as necessary.

7. You may choose to do the 9 gamut or the short cut procedure as described below if you still have problems reducing your level of distress down to a 1 or a 0.

In the 9 Gamut Procedure, you must first locate the gamut point on the back of either hand, 1/2 inch beyond the knuckles (toward the wrist), and in line with the midpoint between the pinky finger and the ring finger. While constantly tapping the gamut point, do the following nine actions:

1. Close eyes.
2. Open eyes.
3. While holding the head still, shift eyes to lower left.
4. While holding head still, move eyes to lower right.
5. Roll eyes clockwise 360 degrees while keeping head still.
6. Roll eyes counter-clockwise 360 degrees while holding head still.
7. Hum a few bars of your favorite tune for a few seconds (e.g., "Somewhere Over the Rainbow", "Happy Birthday," "Row, Row Your Boat.")
8. Count to five.
9. Hum once again.

OR try the short version by tapping on your gamut spot while holding your head straight and moving only your eyes down to the floor and then up toward the ceiling.

As you repeat these treatments over time, the negative feeling or shadow thought should go away.

5. Applying Key 6:

Example 1: Jeanette is a 50-year-old married female whose husband was an extremely controlling and at times an emotionally abusive man. Jeanette had worked for years in the helping profession as a social worker and had done a great deal of work with women who had been in abusive relationships. She was an incredibly compassionate woman who had focused primarily on taking care of her clients, her children, her husband and her family. She had neglected, however, to focus on her own needs or on self-nurturance. She had a strong belief that had been entrenched since childhood that other's needs were more important than her own.

Jeanette came to me when she was experiencing significant emotional distress when she discovered that her husband had been having an affair that had been going on for a few years. When she confronted her husband, he refused to break off the relationship and confessed that he was very confused about whom he wanted as a life partner, his wife of 25 years or this new woman in his life who was younger, demanding and very materialistic. Jeanette came to further discover that her husband had been essentially supporting this other woman's family – paying off her credit cards, paying for her children's extracurricular activities, and giving her children expensive gifts – while at the same time neglecting his own family's finances.

I was perplexed by Jeanette's continued view of compassion toward her husband. She wanted her husband to be given the chance "to sort things out and make a choice" yet seemed reluctant to have a similar compassionate view toward herself. She seemed to have more concern for "rocking the boat" due to her husband's position in the community as a prominent businessman. She also had a great deal of concern about the wellbeing of her four school aged children. Jeanette talked her husband into pursuing marital therapy, yet was dismayed when he refused to discuss any issues of major concern in the sessions with their therapist. Yet she still seemed reluctant to "rock the boat" although she was terribly unhappy.

As a child Jeanette had made a pact with herself that she would "never consider divorce" since her parents had split up when she was quite young. Yet in her current situation she felt so disrespected by both her husband and her self. She felt so trapped. The final straw on the proverbial camel's back was when her eldest child began to come to Jeanette and question the relationship between her father and this new woman in their lives. This was a defining moment for Jeanette to decide to become unstuck.

I encouraged her to consider a unique approach. We discussed the 12 Keys and she began putting them into practice in her daily life. The experience of Key 6 was particularly powerful for Jeanette. Her realization that her needs WERE as important as anyone else's was a pivotal moment for her. She began to use all of the 12 Keys to heal her self from all the perceived hurts she had experienced.

Jeanette realized that she was a role model in every sense for her children; and she needed to lead by example, not only displaying compassion toward others but also compassion toward self and demonstrate a high level of self-respect. She found that her capacity for compassion and love expanded even further when she began to take the time to nurture herself, and she actually was more present to be compassionate toward her clients. Jeanette also learned to set better limits on what she would and would not permit in her life and in her social work practice. She began to cull her practice down to only see clients who had a sincere desire to get out of being stuck in their lives.

She began to exercise regularly and learn Tai Chi. Shortly thereafter, she finally set limits with her husband by letting him know what she would and would not tolerate in the future. When her husband continued to refuse to shift his perceptions or to actively make a choice him self to recommit to their relationship, she did the only compassionate thing she could for herself and her children; she filed for divorce.

Jeanette and her children have blossomed, been happier, and more at peace since she acted on that decision one and one-half years ago. In Jeanette's own words: "The hardest lesson I have ever had in my life is the lesson of self-love. It has been the most painful and yet the most powerful and shifting one in my life. I recommend it highly."

Example 2: Denise is a 48-year-old married female who has suffered from chronic Post-Traumatic Stress Disorder due to severe childhood physical and sexual abuse. When I first met Denise, she had been treated with medication for both depression and anxiety; and she had already actively participated in intensive group and individual psychotherapy for ten years. When she came to see me for evaluation, she was still actively having symptoms of flashbacks of past traumas, nightmares, almost daily panic attacks, depression and fibromyalgia.

Due to her horrendous childhood experiences (including a particularly brutal sexual assault under a Christmas tree), she was unable to tolerate holiday decorations and avoided all retail stores from mid-October until late January throughout her adult life. Denise had come to the belief that nothing would ever help her heal completely from her past. She had come to believe what she had been told over the years, that she would have to just learn to live with her symptoms that she would have for the rest of her life. While she was very skeptical that the 12 Keys would be able to help her any more than her intensive treatment in the past had, Denise finally decided to open herself up to the possibility that the teachings, tools and techniques might just help her cope a bit better – especially since the holiday season was rapidly approaching once again.

While the first 5 keys were helpful to her in diminishing her physical pain from fibromyalgia, assisting her with realizing how much love was available to her in her life, and realizing her incredible strength and power; it wasn't until she experienced the teachings, tools and techniques above in Key 6 that she truly began to shift. It is said best in her own words:

"I was at first not sure about this 12 Keys course. I did not feel 'ready' for reasons unknown to me. I feel so blessed that I did because of what not only I learned, but how I feel and I think I act differently. I've learned to think (most of the time) before I react. I seem to have more peace, energy, self-worth and an excitement about life. I can see things more clearly. A lot of things I have carried around for forty plus years like shame, abandonment, fear, guilt and just plain sheer gut-wrenching pain at times. I am slowly letting go of some of these and becoming a happier person. I have definitely grown mentally. Before the 12 Keys I got my feelings hurt or stepped on a lot. The 'inner child' I held inside dictated a lot of my emotions like fear, hurt and dread. I feel now I am able to let go of some and start to 'grow up'. I have always been very spiritual – that is one reason I think I survived my childhood – but my scope on spirituality has very much broadened now. I'm learning to accept life (past and present) more, which I can accept as wisdom and learning. I didn't realize that I was such an angry and controlling person before. I still am to a degree. Forty plus years of 'oppression' and I think that's what severe childhood abuse can put you under but I hope to eventually get through anger and control. There are other things about myself and I have to admit (and wouldn't have before) or maybe I didn't realize then about myself I will work on every day. I still feel very blessed most of all that I have a huge capacity to feel love for others and that I feel much pride in being a survivor."

Denise has been putting all of the teachings and tools from the 12 Keys into practice in her life. She now only rarely has a panic attack and she rests well at night without nightmares. She remains on medication for her mood, but her depression is currently in remission. Denise is thrilled that for the past two years, since using the teachings of the 12

Keys, she has been able to go out holiday shopping with family and friends. She actually finds the holiday decorations to be very beautiful and heart-warming once again – an experience she hasn't had since she was 5-years-old; and she has decorated her own Christmas tree in her home for the first time in her adult life. She is finally beginning to establish her own joy-filled holiday traditions with her own children.

KEY 7. The Obstacle of Inadequacy and Powerlessness

We all have crises at some point in our lives. They are the tests and challenges that we all face in our daily existence. Some of them are small and seemingly insignificant in the scheme of things such as being late for an appointment or burning dinner in the oven. Some of our tests and challenges loom larger for us, such as a loved one dying, divorce, being fired from a job, a career has lost its reward, a driving dream was not realized, financial problems, children leaving home, children in crisis and we feel helpless, relocation, retirement, or a sudden physical illness. Too often we beat ourselves up when one of these moments arrives, feeling that we have somehow failed or that we are being punished in some manner.

It is important to realize that tests and challenges are part of everyone's life and are a tool for growth, learning and expanding our perspective on our own life. It helps to view tests and challenges as an opportunity to shift and grow. These life challenges allow us to get out of our narrowly defined world of our egos and assist us with becoming aware of whom we really are versus who we are not. It gives us the opportunity to evolve into our greater self and, ideally, to develop more compassion and love for ourselves as well as for others. Or we can remain stuck. The choice is ours -- but recognize the choice is always there.

These challenge moments make us stop abruptly and examine who we really are, what we expect out of life, how we perceive ourselves and how we want others to perceive us. They define our strengths and our perceived limitations. Once we rise to the challenge of the moment, our perspective can expand. We begin to realize that we are not limited by anyone or anything except for ourselves. We are not victims of our circumstance; we are the creators in our daily lives. Whatever thoughts you had yesterday define who you are today, and whatever thoughts you have today define who you will be tomorrow.

We have the opportunity to create our self anew every day. We use our thoughts and feelings about our self and our world to paint the canvas of our lives. A test or challenge is actually a moment of mastery. It is about your choices and the exercise of free will in how you respond to the challenge of the moment. It is an opportunity to create from your intention and to not be a victim of your circumstances. You are very powerful in your choices.

Although it is healthy to have tests and challenges in your life, as they are a tool for growth, it is important to balance these mastery moments with periods of relaxation, peace and enjoyment. You need to consciously make time in your daily life to rejuvenate and restore your self. This may be done by spending time in nature, meditation, exercise, pursuing passionate hobbies, playing, and doing other joyful activities. We will address this issue in Key 10.

The following exercises can be helpful for finding your center during a test or challenge; and they can assist with reconnecting you with your inner strength, dignity and unity with all that is once more during those mastery moments.

Rising to the Challenge Exercises:

1. Mountain Meditation:
Hint-This meditation will be more effective if you have a friend read it with feeling to you or you record yourself reading it with heart on an audio tape and play it back to follow as you meditate in a quiet private space. This meditation can also be found on a companion CD that accompanies this book (for details see www.12keystoshift.com).

Close your eyes. Take a deep breath and as you exhale, feel tension releasing from your body. Take two more slow, deep breaths, and as you exhale, feel your muscles relaxing even more.

Sense yourself walking on a path in an alpine forest. With each step you take feel yourself more present and alert. Be aware of the fresh, clean scent of pine in the air. Although the air is brisk, the gentle warmth of the sun feels so good on your skin. The sky is a beautiful azure blue and you are feeling very connected to nature.

Ahead in the distance you see the most splendid majestic mountain that you have ever seen. The immense bluish purple rock reaches so high and the peak is barely visible in the clouds. This is your mountain. Feel yourself drawn to the base of the mountain and begin your trek upward towards the top. Feel the lightness in your legs as if you are being pulled magnetically towards the top without any effort. Feel your amazement at the ease of this climb as you find yourself halfway up the mountainside.

Stop for a moment, look around and marvel at how far you have already come. It seems that the higher you go up this mountain, the lighter you feel and the easier the journey. You begin the trek once again toward the top and now it feels as if your feet are barely touching the ground. It appears as if you are now gliding toward the peak. You are nearly at the top as you enter the mist of the clouds. Reach out and feel the texture of the clouds as you move them gently out of your way.

Now you can see clearly where you have been, where you are going and how easy it can be. Take a deep breath and breathe in the healing light of the universe and feel a sense of joy and knowing that you can accomplish anything that you set your mind to. Feel the connection with everything as you stand there looking out and surveying the spectacular vista before you.

Feel your connection with the mighty mountain. Feel your feet deeply and firmly rooted. Know that you ARE this mighty mountain, strong and majestic. Just as the mountain has been here for eons experiencing the changes of seasons, weather, wildlife and environmental change with time, you too are long lasting and have experienced and endured various obstacles, environmental change and the passage of seasons in your own life.

Like the mountain, you too are majestic, solid and still, rooted in the earth, regal, powerful, centered, and strong. Just as the mountain, you too are beautiful just as you are, whether you are seen by people or animals, whether you are covered by snow in the winter, green in the summer, wrapped in clouds, shrouded in fog, dry or wet. As you sit, majestic and dignified, the world continues to change.

The sun comes up in the morning, reaches its zenith, and sets in the evening. The clouds come and go in the sky. Through all of these changes, you remain solid, rooted and dignified. Any test or challenge in your life is but a brief storm with a beginning, middle and an end. The warmth of the sun will return and new life will emerge once again. Feel your strength, your dignity. Be aware of your long-lasting inner strength and beauty.

Now take another deep breath and feel your connection once again with all that there is in this ever-changing universe. Know that you are part of this whole and that your strength will endure any change or season in your life. Spend as much time as you like on the peak of your mighty mountain.

When you feel you are ready to return to your physical world, feel yourself making the return journey from your mountain with ease, and gently open your eyes.

2. Connecting Heaven and Earth Exercise:

Begin with your arms at your sides with fingers extended on your thighs and take two deep breaths. Now inhale slowly and deeply as you lift your palms to the center of your chest. Place your hands together in a prayer position as you exhale slowly. Inhale slowly and deeply once again as you lift one arm and your eyes toward heaven with your palm facing up while at the same time extending the other hand down toward earth with your palm down. As you slowly exhale, bring your hands back to center in the prayer position.

Repeat the above, but this time stretching the alternate arm toward heaven and the other toward earth as you inhale slowly (i.e., if you started with your right arm lifted toward heaven, you would now lift the left arm). Visualize yourself gathering energy from the earth and projecting it toward heaven as you stretch. Repeat the sequence 5 times.

This is a great Tai Chi exercise to get your energies moving and balanced. It helps to distribute the stagnant excess energies that collect in our bodies. This exercise also energetically assists with manifesting the desire to become "as above, so below, perfectly balanced".

3. Connecting Central and Governing Meridian

This daily self-care exercise assists us in feeling our personal power and to be more fully present in our daily life. This technique connects two major energy meridians, one in the front and the other in the back of the body. It also links up the lower three chakras with the upper four chakras. The procedure is performed as follows:

Place the middle finger of one hand in your navel and the middle finger of your other hand on your third eye (in the center of your forehead). With light pressure, gently pull upwards with both fingers and hold for about a minute.

4. Energy Medicine Techniques:

1. Hydrate and do the 3 thumps before proceeding.

Recall a time when you felt that you just couldn't attempt to accomplish a task or get over a particular test or challenge. On a scale from 0 (none) to 10 (most) evaluate the level of distress the following statements provoke before your tapping session so that you can note improvements.

2. Treat the possibility of reversal by repeating one (or any that strongly resonate with you) of the following phrases three times with feeling while tapping on the KC point (if you want to be more specific for your situation, then by all means modify them; phrases you don't use now you can use in subsequent rounds):

"Even though I don't feel strong enough to face (fill in the blank), I deeply and completely love and accept myself and all my feelings."

"Even though I feel helpless, stuck (fill in specific feeling) and I don't know how to move forward, I deeply and completely love and accept myself."

"Even though I have never gotten over my anger (fill in specific feeling) from my divorce, death of my loved one, failed exam, missed meeting, breakup with … (fill in your own test and challenge), I completely love and accept myself anyway with all my feelings."

"Even though I am too afraid to take the first step and rise to the challenge of…(fill in the blank), I choose to completely love and accept myself anyway with all of my feelings."

"Even though it doesn't feel safe to accomplish this because what would others think about me (fill in your circumstance example: my brother would be jealous), I choose to completely love and accept myself anyway."

"Even though if I show my strength and succeed others will be hurt and won't know what to do, I choose to completely love and accept myself with all my feelings."

"Even though I feel helpless to (be specific) and have no control anyway, I deeply love and accept myself with all my feelings."

"Even though I am afraid of failure and know I am not capable of getting over this situation (be specific for your case), I deeply and completely love and accept myself with all of my feelings."

3. Then tap on the following points seven times while thinking about whichever statements above gave you the biggest buzz or level of distress: EB, SE, UE, UN, Ch, CB, UA, and TH.

4. Once again rate your feeling on a 0 to 10 scale. If there is no significant decrease in the rating, go back to step 2 and do 3 more rounds of tapping with feeling. Be sure you are emotionally tuned in to the problem. You may utilize the 9 Gamut Procedure/ sandwich technique if you continue to have difficulty diminishing the limiting belief.

5. In the event you still have no results, look for another phrase, which resonates more for you, reword step two with the new phrase and do 3 more rounds of tapping.

6. As long as your level of distress continues to decrease, keep tapping until there is little or none left. If the treatment still stalls, try tapping on your KC point and say three times with feeling: "Even though I still have some of these feelings or beliefs, I deeply and completely love and accept myself" and do some more rounds of tapping. Repeat as necessary.

7. You may choose to do the 9 gamut or the short cut procedure as described below if you still have problems reducing your limiting belief down to a 1 or a 0.

In the 9 Gamut Procedure, you must first locate the gamut point on the back of either hand, 1/2 inch beyond the knuckles (toward the wrist), and in line with the midpoint between the pinky finger and the ring finger. While constantly tapping the gamut point, do the following nine actions:

1. Close eyes.
2. Open eyes.
3. While holding the head still, shift eyes to lower left.
4. While holding head still, move eyes to lower right.
5. Roll eyes clockwise 360 degrees while keeping head still.
6. Roll eyes counter-clockwise 360 degrees while holding head still.
7. Hum a few bars of your favorite tune for a few seconds (e.g., "Somewhere Over the Rainbow", "Happy Birthday," "Row, Row Your Boat.")
8. Count to five.
9. Hum once again.

OR try the short version by tapping on your gamut spot while holding your head straight and moving only your eyes down to the floor and then up toward the ceiling.

As you repeat these treatments over time, the negative feeling or shadow thought should go away.

4. Applying Key 7:
Example 1: Charles is a 42-year-old male who decided to take the 12 Keys course after being told by his wife "without warning" that she desired a marital separation. He felt overwhelmed and powerless in the situation as well as feeling inadequate in assisting his two young sons with navigating the disruption and turmoil in their lives. He was experiencing significant anxiety and insomnia. He essentially described himself as being paralyzed with fear; he felt completely alone and incapable of tackling the situation he was now faced with.

In the evening after Charles completed the 12 Keys course, he spent a few hours in meditations that he had been taught during the 12 Keys classes. The following is an excerpt from a letter that he sent the day after he completed his meditations dealing with his life crisis:

"Dr. Tracy, I just wanted to say thank you and let you know how much this week has meant to me and helped me. I am sure that you understand this already, but I wanted to say: I never knew that peace was so close and so easy to find. All of my life I have been religious and believed in God. However, in the back of my mind I kept saying that until I saw something that I could touch and feel I would always have doubt. That has now happened. Thank you!"

"I need to share with you what happened tonight. I will try to keep it short. I pictured all of us from the class as I prepared to go into my meditations. This really helped. It was like I was drawn to different ones of the meditations you taught us. I went to work on my anger over the situation like you taught in Key 4 and was told within to 'do it again and this time to make it count'. I then headed for a visit to my True Essence (Key 5) to remind myself of my gifts and abilities to help with dealing with the separation. Then I went to work on my heart and all the heartache I was feeling, like you taught in Key 8. When I did the mountain meditation, I began to feel my inner strength and power once again to cope with this separation from my wife. I began to realize that I could and would weather this 'season' in my life -- as would my children."

"Then I decided it was time to go to the Temple of Wisdom as you taught us to do in Key 9. During this time the energy I felt became so strong in my face that it was almost hurting. While in the Chamber of Wisdom I asked why my face was nearly hurting and was told pretty much that I needed to set things right with my wife and clear the air before I could move on with anything. In addition, Jesus was there in the Chamber of Wisdom with me and assured me that he would always be there with me. To prove it, he even left the chamber with me. When I came out of the Chamber of Wisdom, there was a gift waiting on the table for me, a crucifix for me to keep. I watched as light came down from above and Jesus went up into the light."

"Then I went to the area for Divine Assistance like you taught us in Key 3 and I could see my kids there. The boys sat on my lap. Then I was transported back to the house with my boys. Everyone was asleep. I went to each of my sons, shared my energy with them, and told them that I loved them. Their spirit answered that they already knew. I could see a column of golden light going up from each of their heads. Then I went to my wife's room and shared my energy with her. I even sent some to her lower back where she has problems. I could feel the energy drain from my face as I shared it, but it even became stronger in my hands. I knew I could do whatever I needed to assist us all with making this transition as compassionately as possible. Then, as I went back down the hall, there was a column of golden light that took me back to where I was in the present. Okay, so that was not REAL short, but I wanted to share it with you. Hey there was a lot more, but this is the most important stuff. Thank you again…"

Example 2: Elaine is a 45-year-old female who decided to take the 12 Keys course after she began having anxiety and panic attacks. Her anxiety started after she had a "health scare" following a skin biopsy of a suspicious-looking mole. Even though the results of the test revealed Elaine to be healthy, she continued to experience intermittent episodes of overwhelming anxiety. She had a great deal of stress in her life. She was a wife, a working mother, and also a graduate student, attending a few evening courses each semester toward a masters degree program. She was trying to decide what career path to take upon completion of her graduate studies. She felt like the decision was going to have a huge impact on her whole family and she felt too overwhelmed by the weight of the responsibility to make any decision. She felt stuck.

Upon completion of the 12 Keys, she had the following comments to share:

"The frequency of panic attacks has dramatically been reduced. I 'trust' myself more. With the meditations, I have a place to go that is truly a sanctuary, a place to ask questions, receive answers, and know – without doubt – that I am at the exact place I should be. Tests and challenges are just that – they exist, but I do not fear them as I once did. They are finally contained; I only give them the time and mental attendance they are due, and not a bit more."

"I feel that I have much greater insight that is given to me to use at work, at school, and at home, in all areas of my life. My mental capacity to make connections and to understand what people need and how to give it to them is increased. I am learning at a significantly improved rate. I am able to complete mental tasks with much more efficiency and accuracy. I feel more mentally disciplined."

"The mountain meditation for accomplishment is one of my favorites. I soar; I fly. This is where I feel the most restorative power, as well as direction. I am always provided with the power I need to accomplish the tasks that lay ahead. But it is also much more than that – very spiritual – an interaction with the divine."

KEY 8. The Obstacle of Heartache

Do you recall your first heartbreak? It may have been moving away from your childhood friend, breaking up with your first girlfriend or boyfriend, the loss of a loved one (a pet, family member or a cherished childhood object), or a specific childhood trauma. At the time it occurs and in the days (and sometimes years) following the heartbreak, it seems as though your heart will never be whole again.

Depending on the intensity of the event, we heal from the acute pain with time, but we learn to guard our heart so that we are not "left so vulnerable" again. This sounds like an excellent solution intellectually; however, building walls around our heart prevents us from allowing love in or out. Guarding our heart inhibits our ability to have truly intimate relationships with others. We cannot feel the love from others – nor are we freely open to give our love and empathy to others in either our casual social relationships or in our more significant relationships in our life. We live in fear and angst of being hurt again due to our past experiences. We anticipate that people in our life will hurt us once again.

We also deal with minor heartbreaks every day in the form of "disappointments". Remember the last time you thought you had made that great score on an exam or evaluation, or were next in line for a promotion at work, or thought you had the great parking space near the front of the huge store during prime shopping season -- only to find out that you didn't? When we experience an accumulation of a series of minor disappointments over time, it can have the same effect on our heart center as a major heartbreak such as a traumatic loss (death, divorce, etc.). Therefore, it is important to mindfully focus on our heart regularly to allow our heart to heal from the daily wear and tear of our life drama.

The importance of mindfully healing the heart center daily must be emphasized. Whenever we set our intention to heal our own body or set our intention to send healing to others, the creative force to manifest the healing flows first through our own heart. In fact, the power to create or manifest anything with great love and joy (positive abundance or heaven on earth) lies in a free and flowing heart center. If we are guarding our heart, we inhibit the ability to manifest positive abundance in our life.

As painful as some of our life experiences can be at times, it is important to be aware that our heart is never truly "broken". We all have a never-ending capacity to receive and to express love even though some may believe they have never felt it in their life experience. It is actually our ego and our mind that respond to the perceived insult of experiences that take place in our outer world. We, in our humanness, tend to interpret other people's actions, thoughts and feelings as reflecting something about us that defines who we are. In fact, we are not responsible for anyone else's thoughts, feelings or actions. THEY are. WE are responsible for our OWN thoughts, feelings and behaviors. We cannot change anyone except for our self. We can, however, change how we choose to respond to others.

We can choose to shut down our heart and closely guard it, expecting that everyone we meet will cause us more heartbreak. OR we can make a choice to expand our heart, be more fully present in the moment and allow our love, passion and joy to flow in our life and in our relationships. The following exercises can assist with allowing your heart center to heal so that you may feel the flow of love more fully in your life.

Exercises for Healing Your Heart from Heartbreak or Disappointments:

1. Healing the Heart Meditation:

Hint- This meditation will be more effective if you have a friend read it with feeling to you or you record yourself reading it with heart on an audio tape and play it back to follow as you meditate in a quiet private space. This meditation can also be found on a companion CD that accompanies this book (for details see www.12keystoshift.com).

Close your eyes. Take a deep breath and as you exhale feel all of your tension releasing from your body. Take two more slow deep breaths and each time you exhale feel your muscles relax more and more.

Picture yourself walking down a beautiful path in a lush tropical forest. It feels so good to have this time for yourself. Soak in the colors, sounds, scents and textures of nature surrounding you, using all of your senses. Be aware of each step you take as your foot connects with the earth while you walk slowly down this path. As you walk along further, notice how the path gradually widens in front of you to reveal a beautiful white sandy beach.

When you reach the beach, take off your shoes and allow the soles of your feet to be caressed by the texture of the fine sand. Feel the weight of your body being absorbed by the cushion of sand supporting you, as you walk along the beach towards the water. Feel the warmth of the sun and the soft ocean breeze on your skin. Be aware of how good it feels. Allow your senses to open fully and be mindful of the fragrance of the salt in the air and the sounds of the gentle waves ebbing and flowing at the shoreline.

Now look out at the crystal turquoise waters of the beautiful calm ocean. As you look out at the horizon you will see the most beautiful, graceful, grey dolphin gently breaking through the water and swimming towards you. Feel yourself stepping into the water, which is warm and inviting. It is time to meet your Dolphin who has come to heal your heart and free your heart from any past or current pain.

Watch as the Dolphin gently swims beside you and lovingly nudges and encourages you to hold onto its fin. Feel the smooth skin of the

Dolphin and allow your Dolphin to take you deeper into the water. Feel the depth of your love flowing to the Dolphin. Be fully present and feel the oneness with your Dolphin. Now sense the joy and unity as your Dolphin playfully moves through the beautiful emerald colors of the water. Feel your self, gliding freely in the water, afraid of nothing. Feel the water flowing through your heart, cleansing and clearing all the debris and pain.

Focus on your heart as you gently glide through the water. Using all of your senses, recognize all those fragments of your heart that were broken and scattered that are now floating in the water before you. Now it is time to set your intention and state out loud: "I am ready to heal my heart. I desire to fully heal my heart of any wounds present or past. I want to be free to love and be loved."

Do you feel a sense of separation? Pick up a fragment of your broken heart floating before you and take it in your hands. Feel all of your feelings of separation dissolving and being healed. Silently state, "I release all feelings of separation" and feel them go. As separation is released, the fragment of heart in your hands begins to glow as it returns to your heart.

Do you feel betrayed? Find another fragment of your heart floating in the water and pick it up. Sense the heaviness in this fragment of heart in your hands. Feel all of your feelings of betrayal dissolving and being healed. Notice the fragment begins to feel less heavy in your hands. Silently state: "I release all feelings of betrayal" and feel them go. As betrayal is released, the fragment of heart in your hands begins to glow and it returns to your heart. Love is returning.

Do you feel disappointment? Find another fragment of your heart floating in the water. Pick it up and hold it in your hands. Feel the weight of this fragment. Feel all of your feelings of disappointment dissolving and being healed. State silently: "I release all feelings of disappointment" and feel them go. As disappointment is released, the fragment in your hands feels lighter and begins to glow as it returns to your heart.

Do you feel sadness? Pick up another fragment of your heart floating before you. Feel all of your heavy feelings of sadness dissolving and being healed. Say silently "I release all feelings of sadness" and feel them dissipate. As sadness is released this fragment of heart in your hands also begins to glow. It returns to your heart. Love is being restored.

Do you feel abandoned? Find another fragment of your heart floating before you in the water and pick it up. Feel all of your feelings of abandonment dissolving and being healed. Say silently "I release all feelings of abandonment." Feel them go. As they do, the fragment in your hands begins to glow and returns to your heart. Love is returning.

Do you feel grief and loss? Find another fragment of heart and gently take it into your hands. Feel the weight of all of your feelings of grief and loss dissolving and being healed. Say silently "I release all feelings of grief and loss." Feel them go. As all feelings of grief and loss are being released, the fragment in your hands begins to glow and also returns to your heart. Love is returning.

Do you feel shame? Find another fragment of your heart floating before you in the water. As you take it into your hands, feel the heaviness contained in this particular fragment of heart. While it appears to be so much heavier than the other fragments, it is only the secret guilt and shame that you have harbored that causes it to seem so much weightier. Feel all of your feelings of shame dissolving and being healed. State silently "I release all feelings of shame". Feel them go and notice how the fragment of heart in your hands feels so much lighter. As shame is released this fragment in your hands too begins to glow, as it returns to your heart. Love is returning.

Look around and find all of the remaining broken fragments of your heart as your Dolphin gently glides you through the water toward them. Be aware of each emotion associated with each fragment of heart that you take into your hands, and release all the feelings that have caused your heart to feel broken. Feel each fragment of heart glowing and returning to your heart as you heal it. Take as much time as you need to completely heal your heart.

SHIFT: 12 Keys to Shift Your Life

Once you sense that your heart is fully healed, feel your heart with all of the fragments now restored become one whole, beautiful, glowing, radiant heart. Feel the power of the warmth and glow of love in your heart once more and feel the strength, confidence and beauty of your love.

Take a deep breath and feel your heart expanding outward. Take another deep breath and feel your heart expanding even more. Your heart is glowing. Feel the power of your radiant heart to give and receive love endlessly and unconditionally.

As your Dolphin gently brings you back to the beach, thank your Dolphin for assisting you with freeing and restoring your heart. Know that your Dolphin will always be there for you to expand and heal your heart anytime you want. Now feel yourself walking back down your path feeling more relaxed, more alert and more aware than you have ever been. When you feel yourself fully in your body, fully present, take a deep breath and gently open your eyes.

2. Experiencing Your "Loving Self":
There are always tests and challenges that arise that will temporarily cause us to feel our heart starting to shut down or feel guarded either out of anger, fear or disappointment. A technique to immediately recover from the sensation that you are shutting your heart down is as follows:

Close your eyes and picture someone that you have a great love for (this may be someone who is deceased or living). If you have difficulty thinking of someone you have a great love for, then you may find that you can think of an animal, pet or some other thing that you have a great love for such as a beautiful sunset, a starry night or your favorite music.

Picture the person or thing that you love as if it were there with you right now. See, sense or feel them being surrounded in a gold and white light and ask that your love bring healing into their body, life or situation. When you do this, you typically feel a sensation of warmth or fullness in your heart, and you can sense your heart expanding outward. You are now experiencing your "Loving Self", the true essence of whom you really are when you allow yourself to step out of the limits of your ego. Continue to allow yourself to experience your Loving Self until you sense your heart open fully.

Now simply bring that sensation of the Loving Self back into your own body and focus on the current test or challenge you are facing from the perspective of your Loving Self. You will find that you may have a positive effect on the person or situation that you are facing when you come from the perspective of your Loving Self. If you do not have a positive effect on the person or situation, you will at least react differently to the person or situation and not take it as personally as you perhaps had before.

3. 4th/Heart Chakra Exercise:
The heart or fourth chakra is located one hand's width above the third chakra in the center of the chest. This energy center resonates with the color emerald green or pink, the tone "ah", and the musical note F or B (you must discern which resonates more strongly for you).

Focus on your heart and set your intention to balance and heal your heart center. With mindfulness, see, sense or feel a column of golden white light coming down from above to the level of your heart surrounding you completely. Close your eyes. Slowly and deeply breathe in some of this beautiful light. Feel the light filling your lungs, entering into your blood stream, and from there traveling to every cell, atom and molecule in your body. As you exhale, feel any negativity within your body being released and leaving you.

Breathe in more of this golden white light and, with each breath, feel your body becoming more and more light-filled until eventually it is completely filled with gold and white light. Once you sense that this has occurred, deeply inhale some of this light directly into your heart but now sense, see or feel the light as being pink in color. Sense this pink light swirling with intention in a circular fashion within your heart chakra, healing any and all imbalances (physical, mental or emotional) within your heart center. Do this as you tone the sound "Ah" to the key of the musical note F or B if you have a musical instrument available. Otherwise, the intention alone of it being to the key of F or

B will suffice. Repeat the exercise as necessary until you feel its healing effect.

4. Energy Medicine Techniques:
a. Hydrate
Do the over energy correction and the 3 thumps before proceeding.

b. Tapping in Positive Affirmations:
Think of the most joyful and loving experiences you have ever had. As you focus on these positive past experiences, feel the fullness in your heart and tap these memories into your third eye. Additionally, you may wish to tap in affirmations three times with feeling that include:
" I give myself permission to love myself"
" I deserve to love and be loved"
"I am free to love and be loved"
"I feel that it is safe to love and be loved"
" I am fully capable of giving and receiving love freely"
" I am worthy of love"
" I don't have to earn love"
Add any other affirmations that apply to you.

c. Special Energy Medicine Maneuvers for Heartache or Heart Issues:
If you are unhappy, heartbroken or in an acute crisis, while thinking about the emotion try any or all of the following:
Tap the heart point at the inside of your pinkie fingernail (side closest to ring finger).
Twist the ends of your little finger (9th point of your heart meridian) and hold.
Tap over your thymus in the middle of your chest, as we do in energy self care.
Tap the crease of your wrist on the little finger side (7th point of your heart meridian).

d. EFT Protocol for Heartache:
In the event that you are still having problems shifting your negative thoughts or feelings, rate your level of distress from 0 (none) to 10 (most imaginable) and treat the reversal by tapping your KC point while stating out loud with feeling any of the following affirmations that apply (or create your own) three times:

"Even though I don't feel I deserve to get over (fill in the blank) I deeply and completely love and accept myself with all my feelings."

"Even though I don't want to be happy, I deeply love and accept myself anyway."

"Even though I will not allow myself to feel (fill in the blank), I deeply and completely accept myself."

"Even though my heart is too damaged to ever love again, I deeply and completely accept myself."

The affirmation should neutralize the problem. You don't have to believe the affirmation for it to work.

Then tap on the following points seven times while thinking about whichever statements above gave you the biggest buzz or level of distress: EB, SE, UE, UN, Ch, CB, UA, and TH.

Once again rate your feeling on a 0 to 10 scale. If there is no significant decrease in the rating, go back and do 3 more rounds of tapping on your issue with feeling. Be sure you are emotionally tuned in to the problem. You may utilize the 9 Gamut Procedure/ sandwich technique if you continue to have difficulty diminishing the limiting belief.

In the event you still have no results, look for another phrase, which resonates more for you or come up with your own that is more applicable to your particular situation, and do 3 more rounds of tapping.

As long as your level of distress continues to decrease, keep tapping until there is little or none left. If the treatment still stalls, try tapping on your KC point and say three times with feeling: "Even though I still have some of these feelings or beliefs, I deeply and completely love and accept myself" and do some more rounds of tapping. Repeat as necessary.

You may choose to do the 9 gamut or the short cut procedure as described below if you still have problems reducing your limiting belief down to a 1 or a 0.

In the 9 Gamut Procedure, you must first locate the gamut point on the back of either hand, 1/2 inch beyond the knuckles (toward the wrist), and in line with the midpoint between the pinky finger and the ring finger. While constantly tapping the gamut point, do the following nine actions:

1. Close eyes.
2. Open eyes.
3. While holding the head still, shift eyes to lower left.
4. While holding head still, move eyes to lower right.
5. Roll eyes clockwise 360 degrees while keeping head still.
6. Roll eyes counter-clockwise 360 degrees while holding head still.
7. Hum a few bars of your favorite tune for a few seconds (e.g., "Somewhere Over the Rainbow", "Happy Birthday," "Row, Row Your Boat.")
8. Count to five.
9. Hum once again.

OR try the short version by tapping on your gamut spot while holding your head straight and moving only your eyes down to the floor and then up toward the ceiling.

As you repeat these treatments over time, the negative feeling or shadow thought should go away.

Applying Key 8:

Example 1:   Bob is a 38-year-old married male executive who experienced significant physical, verbal and emotional abuse from his father from the age of eight until he finally left home to escape the family environment at age fourteen. In his childhood experience the world was not a safe place and even those he loved most created intense heartache. He learned to guard his heart and live in fear. He was going through life in survival mode.

Bob began to develop fearful obsessive thoughts that he was going to contract a terminal illness that would end his life --- something that he could not feasibly protect himself against. He felt out of control. His obsessions worsened significantly after marrying and starting a family of his own in his late twenties. Bob started to develop compulsive, repetitive behaviors as he lived his life increasingly in fear for the safety of himself and his loved ones.

Even though he had a great love for his wife and beautiful children, the effect of creating strong walls around his heart from his childhood disappointments, grief, anger, humiliation and other negative emotions was profound. He began to compulsively buy firearms each time he received a paycheck and stored them in a gun safe at home. He also repetitively checked his body for signs of skin or testicular cancer and it began to have an effect on his job, marriage and family life.

Although he was a highly intelligent, capable and competent businessman, his climb up the corporate ladder was stalled and his job was in jeopardy. He lost several potential business deals due to reluctance to travel to business meetings by air. He had a fear of getting on planes out of concerns that it might crash. He would have to leave the room if anyone in a meeting mentioned anyone with a terminal illness, even if it was in casual conversation. He got to the point where he would leave work in the middle of the day to go home to have his wife physically examine his body several times in order to reassure himself that he was healthy and cancer-free. He refused to go outside to do yard work without wearing long sleeves, long pants, gloves and a wide-brimmed hat for fear of sun exposure; and he had never taken his family to a beach for fear of developing skin cancer. He found that commercials for sunscreen products or news stories on the rise of skin cancer on television or radio were triggers to intense anxiety and a need to check himself for cancer yet again.

He initially presented to this author for psychiatric treatment when his wife was at her wits end, as she could no longer reassure Bob that he was safe and healthy. He had developed an exercise compulsion and an obsessively strict diet to attempt to defend him self from any potential colon cancer as well. His children had grown to an age where they had begun to ask, "What is wrong with daddy?" He was reluctant to be started on medication to treat his obsessive-compulsive disorder (OCD) due to intense fear of medication side effects. He finally agreed to a trial of a medication to decrease his acute overwhelming anxiety symptoms so that he could make it through a day at work without feeling so panic-stricken, but he made it clear that he wanted this to be a short-term solution. He showed only partial improvement in his acute anxiety symptoms with initiation of a serotonin-specific reuptake inhibitor antidepressant medication (used for OCD) and a low dose of a benzodiazepine (a mild tranquilizer).

He was also open (although skeptical) to pursuing alternative and complementary healing modalities to assist him with transforming his anxiety without reliance on medications. Initially, Bob was hesitant to pursue any approach that would take him away from his family, even for a day, out of angst that he would miss the opportunity to spend that one day with his wife and children in the event that he did eventually die in the near future from a terminal illness. His wife, however, rapidly pointed out to him that he was never fully present with either her or their children when he was at home because he was so constantly preoccupied with his obsessions and compulsive behaviors. He decided to participate in a two-day meditation course offered by us, so that he could learn tools to decrease his angst and improve his home life.

On the morning of the first day of the class, Bob arrived half an hour early and was skeptical but eager to begin his journey. He was fairly relaxed when he arrived. Just prior to the start of class, however, there was a late arrival who showed up with band-aids across her nose and neck. She apologized for her appearance but explained that she had had two suspicious skin lesions biopsied the day before by her dermatologist, and she was awaiting to hear if they were cancerous or not.

As you can imagine, this sent Bob into a full-blown panic with acute anxiety/fear, chest tightness, shortness of breath and his hands began to shake uncontrollably. His voice became tremulous as beads of sweat popped out on his forehead. The fear in his eyes was intense as he whispered, "I've got to go… I need to call my wife." The start of class was delayed as his wife was contacted by phone and Bob was encouraged to stay for the class. He finally admitted that, if he left at that moment, then he would likely never come back for another class in the future. Still shaking, he agreed to try to stay for the class, but he made it clear he might still have to leave. He was petrified.

Having to face his fears directly in the class while learning to release his fears was crucial for him. His transformation over the next two days was remarkable. He was able to heal his heart from past childhood wounds that caused him to live in a chronic state of fear that he and his family would not be safe.

In his own words: "This was a great experience. My panic and anxiety are gone. After 15 years of psychotherapy, lots of meds, and lots of money, I have finally found a way to make panic, OCD, anxiety go away. It works; I was skeptical, but it really does work." "I will always have perfect health, family love, security, money, and no worries."

Since his transformation, Bob is able to travel for his work, is now the most successful salesman in his region, is scheduling vacations with his family in tropical spots, and is more fully present with his wife and children. His coworkers have noticed an enormous difference in him and want to know what he is doing differently as they now want to emulate him. He has been able to decrease some of his psychotropic medication and is experiencing more joy in his daily life. His children have their father back once again.

Example 2: Mary is a 47-year-old married female writer who experienced childhood emotional abuse by her father. She was stalled in her pursuit of joy and sense of purpose after a traumatic event that occurred while on a small sailing vessel at sea in the Antarctic with five other adults. During the trip she befriended a younger woman named Chris who became acutely ill on the ship and died. They had to bury Chris' body at sea and Mary was the one who had comforted Chris as it became increasingly obvious that she would never make it home to her family and friends. Mary was haunted by her sense of heartbreak and responsibility to share this woman's story yet felt helpless to heal herself or to empower herself to write this woman's story as she had deep feelings of unworthiness.

Mary felt that her heart was too wounded from the pain of her brief encounter with Chris to effectively handle her own emotions. She felt such grief over losing someone with whom she had felt such a rare, brief, and yet intense connection. Mary also found herself replaying the old negative tapes in her head from her father's emotionally abusive comments to her in childhood as she focused on her unworthiness to write such a profound story. She found herself drowning in her own sea of heartbreak and could find no way out.

Mary took part in an intense weekend course taught by these authors that gave her the tools and techniques described in Key 8. Her experience in her own words is as follows:

"I am flat-out happier; I have a joy that has been missing since childhood. I give myself permission to be me everyday. I feel accepted by the spiritual beings in my life; therefore, my concern for what those here on the planet think is in correct proportion. Even what I think is less pertinent. I have laughter in my head constantly! It is great fun. I've had lots of emotional tests and challenges, but I have been given a delightful poker face so that when interacting with angry or aggressive people, I am able to giggle on the inside, and maintain a façade that gives away little – my face used to provoke agitation in others. I reflected everything I thought: now, I reflect much less that produces a negative reaction. What emotion I do show seems much more appropriate and results in a more positive outcome."

Mary is now more fully present in her daily life. She is joyfully experiencing and expressing her love in her life and in her relationships. She has begun to write a book detailing the memoirs of the deceased young woman Chris whom she befriended and bonded with so closely. She has a knowing that it is her purpose to write this story for others. Her husband and children are very supportive of her endeavor.

Key 9: The Obstacle of the Unknown

One of the greatest fears of humans is the fear of the unknown. Many people remain stuck in their circumstance for fear of taking a different path or direction that is unknown to them. Universal Wisdom is the knowledge and experience needed to make sensible decisions and judgments that are applicable to all situations or purposes. Essentially it is the ability to "see the big picture" of any situation or experience in your life and not take any situation personally. When you see the big picture you see everything from a different perspective and gain the understanding that everything happens for a purpose and that nothing is random. You begin to understand that all life experiences assist us with understanding more of who we are and who we are not. If we do not understand the lesson that we draw to ourselves, we will continue to create a similar life lesson until we do understand it. Therefore, it is important to learn how to go within and ask what the lesson to be learned is from any given situation or crisis that is present or has occurred in your life.

What prevents us from accessing Universal Wisdom when we need it the most? What keeps us from being able to see the big picture? Most often it is our overwhelming emotions during a crisis or situation in our life that keep us from having clarity. We can't see the forest for the trees. How do we tap into our inner wisdom? First, it is important to transform the anger, resentment, fear and heartbreak over the issue in order to be still and become aware of the small inner voice that gives us answers to all situations. The exercises and meditations in Keys 4 and 8 in this book will assist with shifting anger, resentment, fear and heartbreak. Keys 1 and 2 will assist if there are overwhelming feelings of unworthiness, guilt or shame that are preventing you from gaining clarity.

Essentially, all of the previous Keys in this book prepare you for getting out of your own way so that you may be able to feel worthy of and experience the wisdom of the still, small voice of the teacher (True Essence) within us all that already knows where we have been, where we are now, and where we are going. The teacher within us all is aware that everything is in Divine Order every moment of every day. There is nothing "unknown" to our inner teacher; and our True Essence will never frighten us. Our wise inner teacher is never punishing and never sees us as a failure. Our True Essence is compassionate and loving at all times.

The following exercises will assist you, when you are ready, with experiencing the Universal Wisdom that is always available to you. They will allow you to "see the big picture" of every situation and circumstance in your life.

Exercises for Tapping into Universal Wisdom:

1. Temple of Wisdom Meditation:
Hint- This meditation will be more effective if you have a friend read it with feeling to you or you record yourself reading it with heart on an audio tape and play it back to follow as you meditate in a quiet private space. This meditation can also be found on a companion CD that accompanies this book (for details see www.12keystoshift.com).

Close your eyes. Take a deep breath; and, as you exhale, feel your body relaxing and all muscle tension beginning to leave your body. Take two more slow, deep breaths and as you exhale feel yourself relaxing more and more.

Picture, sense or feel a column of golden white light coming down from above you, surrounding you and filling you. Breathe in some of this golden white light. Sense it going into your lungs, from there entering your bloodstream, and traveling around to every cell, atom and molecule of your body. As you exhale, sense any negativity leaving you. Take two more slow, deep breaths of this beautiful golden white light and feel your body becoming completely filled with light.

As you take another slow, deep breath, see, sense or feel yourself beginning to lift up within this beautiful column of golden white light. With each intake of breath, sense yourself lifting up higher and lighter, lighter and freer, and freer and higher within the column of light. Feel yourself lifting higher and higher within the light until you begin to sense, see or feel a more brilliant light that draws you toward it.

As you enter this radiant light, you become aware of another dimension before you that seems so familiar. Up ahead, you see a pyramid of light with an eye above it representing all of the knowledge of the universe that is available to you. As you draw closer to this pyramid of light, you become aware of a doorway. This is your Temple of Wisdom. Above the arched doorway of this temple is a symbol of an ancient scroll that represents ancient wisdom.

As you enter the door of the temple, there are two small stone tables on either side of the entranceway. On the table on the left you will find three beautifully shaped crystals. One is pink and represents Unconditional Love. One is gold and represents Divine Wisdom. One is blue and represents Divine Assistance.

Now look toward the table on the right. On this table you will find a crystal key. This is the Key of Universal Wisdom. This key will unlock the door to the Chamber of Wisdom and will give you the ability to access the answer to any question regarding any situation in your life. Pick up the Key of Wisdom and move it around in your hand. Remember, this key will help you answer any question.

Walk toward the back of the temple and you will find a golden door. This door leads to your Chamber of Wisdom. To the right of the door stands a beautiful black panther that represents the fear of the unknown. Look into the panther's golden, almond-shaped eyes and feel the absolute acceptance and unconditional love that is emanating from the panther toward you. Feel the inner peace and tranquility that it brings to feel all that love flowing toward you.

Send your love back to the great, black panther and reach out to stroke the velvet coat of this sleek animal. Sense yourself being surrounded by love from this mystical creature. Now see, sense or feel yourself stepping even closer to this beautiful animal and feel yourself throwing your arms around this mighty feline and embracing the black panther. Feel the strength, love, and power flowing through you. Feel any fear or anxiety within you melting away and sense an even deeper inner peace.

Stand once again in front of the door to the Chamber of Wisdom. Feel the Key of Wisdom in your hand and the love of the black panther flowing to you. Inside the chamber you will find a crystal-lined room filled with ancient books containing all of the wisdom and knowledge of the universe. You will also find a very comfortable chair in the center of the room.

Unlock the door and place the Key of Wisdom over your heart. Open the door and explore the room. Feel the wisdom within this room. Take a seat in the chair. Get comfortable. Close your eyes, take a deep breath and as you exhale, allow yourself to completely relax. Feel the love of the black panther and of the universe flowing to you and feel the wisdom surrounding you.

Ask your self the following question: "What is the first thing I must do to bring more love and joy into my life?" Be still and listen for the answer (you may hear an answer, sense an image or picture of the answer, or the answer may just suddenly come to you). Once more, "What is the first thing I must do to bring more love and joy into my life?" Be still and listen.

Once you have become aware of the answer, ask whatever other questions that you desire regarding your life, be still and listen for the answer. Take as much time as you need in your Chamber of Wisdom. Know that you have access to this chamber whenever you need clarity in your life.

When you are ready to leave your Chamber of Wisdom, simply get up from the chair, leave the room, lock the door, and return your key to the stone table inside the doorway of your temple. You may find that you have a gift from your True Essence on the table when you return the key. This gift is to remind you of your loving spirit and may give you further insight into a question that you asked in your chamber or into a situation going on in your life. Open the gift and see what it is; understand the gift's meaning. If you have difficulty understanding, then close your eyes and simply ask, "What is the meaning of the gift?" and then listen for the answer. Once you understand the gift, place it in your heart for you to keep with you always.

Now walk out of your Temple of Wisdom. Feel yourself returning slowly and gently back down the column of light, back to your physical world. When you feel your self fully present in your body, gently open your eyes.

2. 6th Chakra/Third Eye Meditation:

The 6th chakra or Third Eye is located in the center of the forehead, the place where baptismal rituals or anointments are typically performed. The issues linked with this chakra include intuition, spiritual vision, the ability to "see the big picture", clarity, and the senses of vision and hearing (spiritual and physical). The third eye is associated with the color indigo blue, the tone "A", and the musical notes A or E (you must discern which resonates for you).

Close your eyes. Take a deep breath and feel your muscles beginning to relax. Take two more slow, deep breaths and feel your muscles relaxing even more.

Picture yourself standing outside on a perfectly clear summer evening. The sky is a beautiful indigo blue with brilliant twinkling stars scattered throughout the dark blue sky. Immerse yourself in the beauty of the bright points of light floating within the sea of the midnight blue sky. As you take a deep breath in this wondrous outdoor setting, close your eyes. As you exhale, send your love out to those seemingly endless points of light.

As you sense your heart expanding, you begin to become aware of the image of a stunning golden pyramid of Light standing before you. As you look more closely at this magnificent pyramid of Light, you notice a door on one of the sides. Walk up to the door until you are standing just in front of it. Feel your strength. Open the door and go inside.

You suddenly find yourself in a comfortable chamber surrounded by loving beings of Light emanating love and wisdom toward you. As you look around the circle, one being steps forward and directs a wand of Light toward your third eye in the center of your forehead. You become aware of a warmth and light pressure on your forehead.

Then you begin to sense the vastness of the beautiful indigo night sky flowing into your third eye, awakening your cosmic wisdom. Feel your inner vision awakening to a deeper level than you have ever experienced before. Sense the serenity and joy as you feel the expansion of awareness within your whole being. Stay with this experience for a few moments.

Then, when you are ready, sense yourself slowly returning to your body. When you sense that you are fully present, take a deep breath and gently open your eyes as you exhale.

3. Energy Medicine Technique:
Hydrate and do the 3 thumps before proceeding.

1. Recall a time when you felt little clarity or didn't feel "good enough or smart enough" to have access to your inner wisdom. On a scale from 0 (none) to 10 (most) evaluate the level of distress the following statements provoke before your tapping session so that you can note improvements.

2. Treat the possibility of reversal by repeating one (or any that strongly resonate with you) of the following phrases three times with feeling while tapping on the KC point (if you want to be more specific for your situation, then by all means modify them; phrases you don't use now you can use in subsequent rounds):

"Even though I don't feel smart enough and I feel (fill in specific feeling) and I don't know how to think for myself, I deeply and completely love and accept myself with all of my feelings".

"Even though I don't feel good enough to have any intuition (fill in your own negative thought), I completely love and accept myself anyway with all my feelings."

"Even though I don't believe in intuition, I choose to completely love and accept myself anyway with all my feelings."

"Even though it doesn't feel safe to trust myself, nobody else ever trusted me, I choose to completely love and accept myself with all my feelings."

"Even though if I feel confused, I choose to completely love and accept myself anyway with all my feelings."

"Even though I feel helpless (be specific) to tap into divine wisdom and don't deserve it anyway, I deeply love and accept myself with all my feelings."

"Even though I am afraid of not making the right choice and would rather let someone else tell me what's right, I deeply and completely love and accept myself with all my feelings."

"Even though I do not feel that I am connected enough or spiritual enough to tap into spiritual wisdom, I choose to do so anyway and completely love and accept myself with all of my feelings."

3. Then tap on the following points seven times while thinking about whichever statements above gave you the biggest buzz or level of distress: EB, SE, UE, UN, Ch, CB, UA, and TH.

4. Once again rate your feeling on a 0 to 10 scale. If there is no significant decrease in the rating of distress, go back to step 2 and do 3 more rounds of tapping with feeling. Be sure you are emotionally tuned in to the problem. You may utilize the 9 Gamut Procedure/ sandwich technique if you continue to have difficulty diminishing your doubt.

5. In the event you still have no results, look for another phrase, which resonates more for you, reword step two with the new phrase and do 3 more rounds of tapping.

6. As long as your level of distress continues to decrease, keep tapping until there is little or none left. If the treatment still stalls, try tapping on your KC point and say three times with feeling: "Even though I still have some of these feelings or beliefs, I deeply and completely love and accept myself" and do some more rounds of tapping. Repeat as necessary.

7. You may choose to do the 9 gamut or the short cut procedure as described below if you still have problems reducing your guilt, shame, unworthiness or sense of disconnection from God/Source/Spirit level down to a 1 or a 0.

In the 9 Gamut Procedure, you must first locate the gamut point on the back of either hand, 1/2 inch beyond the knuckles (toward the wrist), and in line with the midpoint between the pinky finger and the ring finger. While constantly tapping the gamut point, do the following nine actions:

1. Close eyes.
2. Open eyes.
3. While holding the head still, shift eyes to lower left.
4. While holding head still, move eyes to lower right.
5. Roll eyes clockwise 360 degrees while keeping head still.
6. Roll eyes counter-clockwise 360 degrees while holding head still.
7. Hum a few bars of your favorite tune for a few seconds (e.g., "Somewhere Over the Rainbow", "Happy Birthday," "Row, Row Your Boat.")
8. Count to five.
9. Hum once again.

OR try the short version by tapping on your gamut spot while holding your head straight and moving only your eyes down to the floor and then up toward the ceiling.

As you repeat these treatments over time, the negative feeling or tail enders should go away.

4. Affirmations:
Now create and tap in affirmations with feeling to assist you in accessing your inner wisdom. You may want to include:

"I trust my intuition."

"Everything is in Divine Order at every moment."

"I see the big picture with absolute clarity in every situation."

Tap on your third eye gently several times as you repeat the above affirmations three times with feeling.

Applying Key 9:

Example 1: Shirley is a 47-year-old married female who came to the 12 Keys course after being diagnosed with breast cancer. She had incredible fear over how she would be perceived by her husband with one less breast. Mutual sexual attraction was an essential element in their marital relationship. She didn't even tell her children about her diagnosis as she wanted to protect them from pain and fear; she led them to believe that she had a minor illness requiring a simple hospital procedure. She had already experienced a complete mastectomy during which she had insisted that her breast be immediately reconstructed against her doctor's wishes. Now she was facing chemotherapy treatments, which most assuredly would lead to the loss of all of her hair. She was struggling with how she would explain her hair loss to her children without frightening them. She decided to take the 12 Keys course just before she was to begin her chemotherapy treatments.

Shirley was so numb from her situation that she had difficulty getting into her heart or in touch with her feelings enough to focus on a meditation without distraction from internal fearful chatter. She initially found the EFT tapping protocols to be much more beneficial for alleviating her fear of the unknown. After several weeks of tapping for her angst 4 to 5 times a day, her anxiety was much reduced and at that point she was able to center herself enough to experience meditation at a profound level.

She was able to finally experience her True Essence and connect with something greater than her body or her ego-based self. She was then able to visit her Temple of Wisdom and gain some insight into her situation. She became aware of how her illness was part of her spiritual journey of understanding her purpose and who she really is. She began to have more compassion for herself, and understood that everything, even major life crises, happens for a reason.

Example 2: Oliver is a 48-year-old male who presented with depression after his wife fell in love with another man and moved out of their marital home. They had 3 young children, one was in preschool and two were of elementary school ages. He was started on antidepressant medication with mild improvement in his mood. However, he was still experiencing insomnia, grief, and excessive worry about what was to become of him and his children. When he found out about the 12 Keys course, he eagerly signed up for it hoping to find some relief from his angst and sadness.

Immediately following his 12 Keys classes, he experienced a powerful series of meditations where he began to get answers to several questions regarding his situation. He did the Loved Ones meditation from Key1 and was somewhat amazed to find his wife as well as both of his wife's parents (one of whom had already died before he had met his wife, Sherry) sending love to him. Both of his in-laws were telling him how grateful they were for him having loved Sherry.

When he did the meditation to transform guilt and shame from Key 2, he was able to transform the cocoon that represented Sherry as well as the cocoon that represented him. He reported the most powerful transformation to be the experience of forgiving himself. Then he found that his mother-in-law walked along with him, holding his hand, as he walked down the path toward the urn (from Key 4) to transform the anger he had toward both Sherry and himself.

Once he had completed the meditation from Key 8 for healing his heart, he journeyed to the mountain (as in Key 7) to rediscover his inner strength for dealing with the marital breakup and the possibility of raising his children on his own. Then he visited his Temple of Wisdom to get more specific answers to his questions surrounding his relationship with Sherry. He was touched once again when he heard how much his wife had loved him and that he needed to allow his wife to go on her own journey now in order to heal what had been in her past from her childhood. He was also told that his children needed him to focus on them. When he left his Chamber of Wisdom, he found a gift awaiting him on the table where the key was placed. It was a band of gold inlaid with three diamonds. It represented the strength of his love and unity with his three children. He was told at that point that they would all be healed from their pain in the future and to trust that everything was indeed in Divine Order.

He reported significant decrease in his anxiety and a lifting of his depression following the above journeys. He was no longer so fearful of his future and the future of his three young children. He began to feel more compassionate toward Sherry in her journey to heal. He began to acknowledge, take appropriate responsibility, and forgive himself for the role he had played in the creation of what had occurred within their marital relationship. He began to realize that neither he nor Sherry had been either demons or saints in what had played out in their relationship. He began to have more clarity and compassion as to how the expectations with which they had each entered their marital relationship had eventually played out in their marital drama and in their lives. He began to understand the value of the lessons that had come out of the relationship with Sherry, including the lessons of forgiveness and compassion.

KEY 10: The Obstacle of Stress

We all need periods of Peace And Restoration (PAR) in our lives to feel a sense of balance, love, community or spiritual connection. PAR is also essential to reduce our stress level. Many of us don't take the time we need to relax, recharge, or express our joy. It is important to give yourself permission and then take the time to do whatever activities bring you PAR on a regular basis.

Do not consider it selfish to carve out a reasonable amount of time for yourself and /or your loved ones to go out and have fun, rejuvenate, relax and disconnect from your stressful daily or weekly routine. It is essential to recharge your battery in some fashion every day to counteract the stress in your life.

We often get so caught up in the fast pace and stress of our daily lives that we no longer feel refreshed and alert enough to really have the clarity to observe where we are and what we have created in our lives. PAR gives us the time and space to best evaluate and envision our intentions so we can create our reality anew from a clearer perspective.

Once you have completed the work of the previous nine Keys, perhaps you will now feel worthy of taking the time to care for your self; and perhaps you will now feel as much compassion for your self as you do for everyone else. Do you get upset if your loved one takes some time to de-stress? Why should it be any different for you to grant yourself the same opportunity? It is time for you to start a regular routine of establishing PAR activities in your life if you have not done so already.

Suggestions for PAR Activities:

Go listen to live music or play an instrument; play a sport or go to your favorite sporting event. Paint, sculpt, take photos, create some form of art or go to an art exhibition or museum and appreciate someone else's creation. If you like to be around the house, you can sew, play cards, mow the lawn, dig in the garden, tend to your flowers, watch the birds, woodwork, or build a dollhouse or a full-scale house. Wash your car with love; or work on its engine. Connect with others; call or visit your favorite family members and friends. Invite friends over or have a party. Write a letter, e-mail or a book.

NOTE: The PAR activities you choose should be enjoyable to you and not a chore. PAR activities are meant to bring a sense of inner peace and joy into your life – not more stress.

Accomplish some fun goals: go float or build your boat (sail or motor); go kayaking, rafting or canoeing; attend a religious service, bask in the sun, go to the gym, meditate, journal; do Tai Chi; take a trip to the book store; take cooking lessons; go back to school. Take a bath. Light a candle.

Engage in some philanthropic activity. Whether it's helping someone mow the lawn, do his or her homework, serve in a soup kitchen, do healing work, or volunteer in a hospital; it can add richness, purpose, and a sense of meaning to our life when we are also mindfully helping others rather than just ourselves.

The list of potential PAR is only limited by your imagination.

Exercise for Increasing your PAR:

Create a list of activities that you feel would bring you a sense of peace, relaxation and inner joy. You may wish to include activities that you have had a passion for in the past but no longer engage in. List activities that you have always wanted to do but have not had the time or resources to do. You can use the list of items above for possible ideas if you are still having difficulty coming up with your own.

Stick to activities that are affordable, attainable and possible. Perhaps flying lessons are out if you are on a budget, but walking in nature, gardening or listening to music is practical for you.

Now write out a monthly calendar of PAR activities, and select a reasonable number of activities to do per week. Schedule when you plan to do them and how you will clear your calendar to make time available. You may find that you just keep putting off your PAR activities if you do not write it out on a schedule and stick to it.

Consider keeping a journal or notebook about your PAR activities. Note in it which activities gave you the most PAR, how each activity made you feel, and how long the positive emotions lasted after each activity. You may wish to plan your schedule of activities for the following month with changes in choices of activities based on your notes.

Rhythmic Breathing Exercise for Stress Reduction:
Rhythmic (or Box) Breathing is a helpful technique for rapidly decreasing stress, anxiety, heart rate or blood pressure. It also is centering and prepares you for a meditation or a peaceful night's sleep.

Think of your breathing pattern as if it were a box or square drawn on a piece of paper with the breathing in being the left upward drawn line, holding your in-breath as the line on the top of the square from left to right, breathing out as the line going downward on the right side, and then the holding of the out-breath being the line from right to left on the bottom side of the square.

You slowly count the length of your breath going in, being held, or going out that is right for you. The length of your in-breath and out-breath should be the same count; just as the length of the held breath at top and bottom should be the same number of counts. As you practice your breathing, you might find that your square is actually a rectangle. Each person may find they have a different count from another person; and that is fine as we are all unique individuals. Just make certain that you are not strained in your breathing in or out or with the breath holds at top or bottom; if you find you are strained, then change the length of your counts for different sides of your "box" of breathing.

Once you find the pattern of your square or rectangular box that works best for you, go through 4 to 5 complete rounds of the rhythmic breathing and notice how your body and mind respond.

Qigong Exercise for Well-Being:
Qigong exercises are used by millions of people around the world for exercise and self-improvement. This ancient practice assists with improving our sense of wellness and vitality, and it also can help us to achieve a sense of inner peace -- thus balancing the body, mind and spirit. Qigong is for people of all ages. There are several books and DVD's available online or at your favorite bookstore.

Here is one of our favorite exercises from Robert Peng, a well-known Qigong master. We recommend his DVD entitled <u>Four Golden Wheels and Lotus Meditation</u> available through his website at *www.robertpeng.com*.

Robert explains that the Four Golden Wheels exercise can assist with balancing the complex network of the energy systems in our body. Doing this exercise daily can improve your sense of peace and wellbeing.

The beginning posture is as follows: With eyes closed or open stand with feet shoulder-width apart, knees bent slightly. Your arms should fall naturally to your sides. Stand with sacrum slightly tucked under your spine as if you were sitting on an imaginary stool. Now stretch your spine comfortably up to the top of your neck, as if someone was gently pulling on a string attached to the top of your head. Keep your shoulders, eyes, face, jaw, and neck relaxed. Imagine that you are opening all the pores of your skin. Smile slightly. Listen for a sound coming from far away. Take deep breaths as you do this exercise.

Bending at the knee begin to very gently shake your body up and down. Keep your body totally relaxed as if you had no muscles or bones. Permit your body to move freely. Connect your mind with all your bodily sensations. Your arms should be loosely hanging at your sides and moving freely and easily. Be as loose as a rag doll. Continue to gently shake your body up and down. With each movement imagine golden light traveling down your body from your head to your toes. As you continue to gently shake your body imagine that your whole body is being completely cleansed of all blocks, illness and fatigue. Feel the perfection of your system. Continue this exercise for a minute or two. Then put your hands on your lower abdomen, relax and breathe deeply.

Energy Medicine Techniques:
1. Zipping Up Your Central Meridian:
This essential daily exercise assists you with feeling strong and centered. It "seals in" your sense of wellbeing and protects you from negative energy coming in from other people or the environment. The electromagnetic energy flowing from your hand moves the energy in the meridian when you perform this exercise.

Place either hand on or just a few inches in front of your pubic bone over the center of your body (the beginning of your central meridian). With intention, breathe in slowly and deeply as you move your hand up the center of your body to the level of the bottom of your lower lip. Repeat this maneuver with your hand three times and, after the third sweep, imagine that you have a key to lock in all of your good energy while keeping out all negative influences.

This is a good technique to protect yourself from all those energy vampires out there who can drain you energetically. It also is a good technique for people who are very empathic and overly sensitive to picking up anxiety or negative vibes from others. You may do this as often as needed throughout the day.

2. The Over-Energy Correction Technique is described in Key 1 as well as in the Appendix. Whenever you feel stressed or overwhelmed, it can rapidly lead to an inner sense of calm.

3. Activating Your Natural Joyful Energies:
Our bodies have a natural joyful energy flow that we can tap into to experience peace and joyfulness. However our chaotic, stressful lifestyles and the high pressures we often experience in Western society have

contributed to us shutting down these joyful energetic circuits. The good news is that we can intentionally reactivate them at any time we choose. Certain body motions can readily open these channels once more. These simple movements can assist you with reawakening your inner natural joyfulness.

a. Figure Eights: Any body movement that creates figure eights will create joyful flows in the body's circuitry. Dance around the room while moving your arms in front of you, either tracing a figure eight or an infinity sign with your body or your arms. Put on your favorite music, relax, and sway your body to the rhythm as you do your figure eights.

Another approach is to trace figure eights on your body or doodle them on paper. When you are feeling stressed out at the office or in a meeting and can't get up to dance, this is a simple solution. Not much equipment is necessary to accomplish this, just the desire to feel joy.

b. Stretching and Energetic Crossover: Any body movement that contributes to stretching can also assist with activating your joyful flows. Recall how delicious it feels to do a complete body stretch when you first wake up in the morning. Movements that cause your energies to cross over your body's midline in addition to stretching, such as tai chi, yoga, swimming, running or walking, also help make space in the body's energy system and open your flows.

For further information on the joyful flows of energy in the body and other techniques for activating them, we highly recommend Donna Eden and David Feinstein's book entitled <u>Energy Medicine</u>.

4. EFT Protocol for Reducing Resistance to Taking Time to De-Stress:
Hydrate and do the 3 thumps before proceeding.

1.Think about a time when you felt guilty or embarrassed that you were taking some time just for yourself for relaxation instead of doing something more "productive". Perhaps you didn't feel worthy of doing something just for you or you were afraid that someone would be jealous if you pursued a certain activity without including them. Maybe you were afraid that you would look lazy if you were not working or appear to be a bad parent if you engage in an activity that does not include your spouse or children. On a scale from 0 (none) to 10 (most) evaluate the level of distress the following statements provoke before your tapping session so that you can note improvements.

2. Treat the possibility of reversal by repeating one (or any that strongly resonate with you) of the following phrases three times with feeling while tapping on the KC point (if you want to be more specific for your situation, then by all means modify them; phrases you don't use now you can use in subsequent rounds):

"Even though there is never enough time for me to take time for myself because (fill in the blank), I choose to deeply and completely love and accept myself anyway with all of my feelings."

"Even though I feel so guilty if I take a hike, go fishing (fill in the blank), I deeply and completely love and accept myself anyway with all of my feelings."

"Even though I don't deserve to go out and have fun, I completely love and accept myself anyway with all my feelings"

"Even though I am afraid that if I stop working, relax and find some joy in my life, I might never go back to work, I choose to completely love and accept myself anyway with all of my feelings."

"Even though I don't want anyone to see me having fun because it doesn't look serious, I completely love and accept myself with all my feelings."

"Even though everyone will judge me for being selfish for leaving my kids (wife…) at home while I (fill in the blank), I choose to completely love and accept myself with all of my feelings."

3. Then tap on the following points seven times while thinking about whichever statements above gave you the biggest buzz or level of distress: EB, SE, UE, UN, Ch, CB, UA, and TH.

4. Once again rate your feeling on a 0 to 10 scale. If there is no

significant decrease in the rating, go back to step 2 and do 3 more rounds of tapping with feeling. Be sure you are emotionally tuned in to the problem. You may utilize the 9 Gamut Procedure/ sandwich technique if you continue to have difficulty diminishing the feeling of guilt, anxiety, etc.

5. In the event you still have no results, look for another phrase, which resonates more for you, reword step two with the new phrase and do 3 more rounds of tapping.

6. As long as your level of distress continues to decrease, keep tapping until there is little or none left. If the treatment still stalls, try tapping on your KC point and say three times with feeling: "Even though I still have some of these feelings or beliefs, I deeply and completely love and accept myself" and do some more rounds of tapping. Repeat as necessary.

7. You may choose to do the 9 gamut or the short cut procedure as described below if you still have problems reducing your guilt, shame, unworthiness or anxiety level down to a 1 or a 0.

In the 9 Gamut Procedure, you must first locate the gamut point on the back of either hand, 1/2 inch beyond the knuckles (toward the wrist), and in line with the midpoint between the pinky finger and the ring finger. While constantly tapping the gamut point, do the following nine actions:

1. Close eyes.
2. Open eyes.
3. While holding the head still, shift eyes to lower left.
4. While holding head still, move eyes to lower right.
5. Roll eyes clockwise 360 degrees while keeping head still.
6. Roll eyes counter-clockwise 360 degrees while holding head still.
7. Hum a few bars of your favorite tune for a few seconds (e.g., "Somewhere Over the Rainbow", "Happy Birthday," "Row, Row Your Boat.")
8. Count to five.
9. Hum once again.

OR try the short version by tapping on your gamut spot while holding your head straight and moving only your eyes down to the floor and then up toward the ceiling.

As you repeat these treatments over time, the negative feeling or shadow thought should go away.

Applying Key 10:

Example 1: Victor is a 47-year-old physician who began to experience mild depression due to the daily stress of trying to balance his busy full-time internal medicine practice with his private life as a husband and father. He also struggled with a long-standing weight issue that he knew was being fueled by his stress level and his resultant attempts to seek comfort in the form of food. He decided to take part in the 12 Keys course after he noted minimal improvement in his mood after starting a low dose of an antidepressant medication.

Now that he has a working understanding of the 12 Keys, he has begun to shift his life. In his own words: "I am working on taking better care of myself. I am more aware of the importance of loving and caring for myself after the course. The meditations and exercises I have learned give me ways to center myself and talk to myself that are healthier than before. The course gave me permission to question, just going with the flow and explore through books and the internet other ways of thinking that are more congruent with my own. I especially use the tools I have learned after a hard day in my medical practice. I also use the techniques and meditations to help me fall asleep. The course exploded my interest in various areas and I have begun to pursue my interests with much more passion. I have also been more compassionate and loving in my relationships with my spouse and children."

Victor has begun to achieve his goal of gradual, healthy weight loss; he no longer follows fad or drastic weight loss protocols. He is just less stressed about his life and no longer feels a need to self-soothe with food. He is no longer taking medication for his mood as he reports feeling "happier and more alive than I have in years".

Example 2: Pam and Ron, a lovely married couple in their early 50's, decided to attend the 12 Keys course following the death of their adult son by suicide. As you can imagine, they were under a great deal of stress from this traumatic event in their family. They struggled with their own emotions (sadness, grief, guilt, shame, fear and resentment) as well as their spiritual beliefs – especially after their pastor told them that their son was most certainly condemned to hell for eternity for having taken his own life. They wished to learn some techniques and tools to help them deal with the intense stress in their lives.

Ron's remarks about what he experienced after taking the 12 Keys course are as follows verbatim: "As you know at the time I took the course I (we) were dealing with the loss of our son (Steve) to suicide. The days you gave to me were at the time a gift from above. To take my mind off of Steve was good. And at the same time to be reassured Steve was okay was so good of a feeling. I needed all that was there. You gave me days of peace! That in itself cannot be evaluated or put into words – you know? I loved my son so much and to think that things in life could lead some one to such is unthinkable, and when I think that you deal with people with bipolar daily, my heart goes out to you. It truly takes a caring person to do the job you do."

"A lot of times I use the meditation where you go up the path and look at the garden and see your loved ones – that's the part I like best. I see Steve among the flowers - but I also see you (?) - I suppose because of the way you showed us how. In a very sincere way I thank you very much for the days of the class. What I remember, I use and it does help mentally. Our home and heart are always open to you! Thank you."

His wife, Pam, had the following to say: "Through meditation and visualization I was able to focus better mentally. This, in turn, affected me physically as I was not so tired because I could sleep better and the stress headaches lessened. I found myself able to be more present and to focus on daily tasks better. I felt calmer; and, when I did feel stressed, the course reminded me to relax and take myself 'away' mentally. This course aided me in my process of becoming more open-minded and accepting all ways of being a spiritual person. The 12 Keys teaches a person to find peace within them selves no matter what life is like NOW. You fill yourself or are filled with an inner calm when using the methods of the 12 Keys."

Ron and Pam decided to use their experiences in dealing with their son's death and their subsequent healing journey to help others. They began a support group for "Survivors of Suicide" to assist anyone who had lost a loved one to suicide. They rekindled a sense of purpose and meaning in their lives once again.

Example 3: Judy is a 45-year-old married female who presented to me for treatment of severe depression and complicated bereavement since the death of her grown son by an unintentional overdose of recreational intravenous drugs. When I first met Judy, her son (Danny) had been deceased for three years; yet she was still actively grieving and intensely angry over her son's death. She still had a living son and a caring husband; however, she remained consumed night and day with thoughts of her deceased son and how much she missed him. She was missing her life and the life of her still living son due to her sole focus on Danny. She was frequently suicidal, tearful, irritable, angry, constantly negative, nihilistic, lethargic, helpless and hopeless. She did not pursue anything that might bring her joy in life because "if Danny can't enjoy anything anymore, then why should I?"

As you can imagine, her depressive symptoms responded poorly to medication and she was somewhat resistant to direct psychotherapeutic approaches. Her husband and younger son were becoming increasingly frustrated and angry with Judy over her behavior and lack of interest in their lives or even her own life. I began to use some of the tools and techniques from the 12 Keys in my work with her, as she was less resistant to guided meditations than she was to actively working in therapy.

She was truly touched by the Loved Ones meditation from Key1, as she was able to actually see Danny there amongst the butterflies and flowers sending her love. She often would use that meditation on her own to visit with or have conversations with her son. She reported that he began to tell her that he was okay now and that he wanted her to take care of his brother.

Her anger was a bit more difficult to deal with initially. Much of her anger was directed toward the drug dealer who had obtained the drugs for her son. It turned out that she knew where he lived; and she admitted to driving past his home at times, seething with anger that he was still alive and enjoying his family while her son was not. She had some difficulty initially releasing her anger until we had used EFT techniques for anger as in Key 4 to prepare her to be ready to release some of it. She has found the "La Cucaracha" Exercise from Key 4 to be helpful to be less affected in her daily life by her anger that she is not yet ready to fully release.

Her most recent hurdle has been allowing herself to pursue any activity that might bring her joy, as she still feels extremely guilty allowing herself to enjoy her life when her son is deceased. We had been discussing PAR activities for her to consider. All she could think of was going into the school system to talk to high school children about staying off of drugs; however, she would become so angry and emotional when she would talk about telling the story of her son that I suggested that she would not be able to be heard by the high school students. They would likely just recall how angry and upset she was and miss the message she wished to convey. She reluctantly agreed that that was probably true. She continued to feel depressed.

When she came in for her last visit with me, she was extremely excited and absolutely full of life. She was no longer depressed for the first time in 3 ½ years. I asked her what had happened to change her demeanor so drastically. She literally looked 10 years younger and she had a huge smile on her face! She explained, "I have found my purpose!" She was out at a coffee shop and happened to see a flier requesting donations and volunteers for an "End of Life Home" in the community.

The small, family-sized home is for indigent people with no families to care for them who have been diagnosed with a terminal illness. In order to be admitted, they must have a life expectancy of less than three months. She had signed up to volunteer and had been in training for it. She reported, "I know that I was supposed to see that flier; I think an angel left it there for me to find!" She will be spending time over the holidays sitting with people who will be so appreciative to have someone, anyone, share their journey with them. She will, in fact, be an angel in their lives.

It is amazing how we humans tend to shine our own Light best and most brightly when we don't just hide our Light inside our own selves; but instead we choose to create an outlet to allow that Light out to leave a trail of Light for others. Judy is now shining her Light brightly rather than just trying to hide it or put it out altogether. Her family is thrilled to have her truly present in their lives once more.

KEY 11: The Obstacle of Habit: Create Yourself and Your Life Anew Every Day

We create very powerfully every day of our lives with our thoughts and our intense emotions/intentions. We create JUST AS POWERFULLY whether we are creating from our shadow (negative, reactive) thoughts or from our true essence (positive, loving thoughts). This is very important to remember because it is so easy to forget this or to overlook this in the often fast pace of our daily lives. It is important to become mindful of the creations you are choosing to send out into the world. It is equally important to censor your shadow thoughts fueled by anger, resentment, fear and anxiety and to actively choose to create from your loving self.

It is easiest to once again visualize this as the Bow and Arrow Theory of creation. The bow represents your intention or the emotional power behind a thought you are sending out into the world. The arrow is the thought itself that you are launching into creation. The arrow will go much faster and further out into the world and manifest more quickly the more powerfully you draw back the bow. If you do not feel strongly about an issue, then you are not pulling the bow back very much at all; and this results in the arrow being launched with very little force. It may create so slowly that you will change your mind and create its opposite effect with more power and more rapidly in the world.

You create MOST rapidly with the strongest emotions or intentions. Thus, what you think about, imagine or focus on today is what you manifest in your life tomorrow. What is manifested in your life today is a reflection of your thoughts, intentions and imagination from yesterday, last week, last month or last year.

Most of the people in our society have no understanding of how powerfully they create. They perceive themselves as victims of the world and blame others for the circumstances in their lives. They often believe that they are doing a wonderful thing by hiding their hostile or angry thoughts and pretending to be kind, generous and loving on the outside to get what they want or manipulate others. However, they are actually creating with the more powerful dark or evil thoughts they harbor inside. Whenever we have conflicting intentions, the stronger one (whether conscious or subconscious) will prevail and manifest.

Why is this Key called the Obstacle of Habit instead of the Obstacle of Creation or the Obstacle of Screwing Up? We are referring to the habit of monitoring thoughts and emotional intentions on a regular basis. Perhaps you recently were one of the billions of people sleepwalking through life, unaware of how powerfully you actually create or draw situations to you every day. If so, then you had a habit of unawareness or unconscious living. Once you have gotten a chance to become aware of who you really are and how powerful you do indeed create in your life, you realize have a CHOICE to create a new habit of conscious daily living or you may choose instead to slip back into the old habit of sleepwalking once more.

It is important that you review your intention (the emotion behind the creation) before you choose to go create consciously in your life. If you are angry, resentful, fearful or anxious, then it is strongly recommended that you review the exercises in the corresponding keys and transform those shadow thoughts fueling the reactive emotions. If you choose not to transform those negative feelings/intentions, then you may unwittingly create disharmony, confusion and chaos in your life.

Exercises to Complete Before Consciously Creating:

***NOTE: This is the only Key where you are well advised to complete the previous Key exercises at least once before you attempt to consciously create in your life. Otherwise your creation may

be affected by negative, shadow thoughts that have not yet been transformed. ***

1. Recognizing Your Shadow Characters and the Roles They Play in Your Life: Whenever we are not in our heart or in our Loving Self, we are essentially in a negative, reactive shadow self creating powerfully from our baser emotions rather than from love. We have a cast of shadow characters within us that can rear their ugly heads. They include: The Furious One, The Scared One, The Cruel One, The Powerless One, The Guilty One, The Pleasing Caretaker, The Sarcastic One, The Sightless One, The Fake One, The Inconsiderate One, The Worthless One, The Secluded One, The Defiant One, The Dissatisfied One, The Evasive One, The Woeful One, The Critical One, The Scheming One, The Obedient One, The Frozen (Numb/Empty) One, and The Confused One.

Think of the last few negative interactions you had with your partner, spouse, children, boss, friend or family member. Replay the interactions in your mind as if you were observing it on a movie screen. Now review the above list of shadow characters and note which ones closely resemble the energy or emotion that you were in throughout various times of the negative interaction that you are recalling. Were you angry? Trying to please others? Anxious? Blind? Cruel? Etc. Be aware of the sequence of shadow characters and the quick costume changes that you did as you shifted from one character to the next. Be aware of how the person you were interacting with also shifted from one shadow character to another. Were you mirroring one another or reflecting off of one another?

For instance, if you started out in your Furious One, then the other person may have responded by shifting into the energy of THEIR Furious One. Then perhaps they became the Critical One and you may have either shifted into your Critical One or perhaps you went to your Guilty One or Worthless One. Begin to become aware of the dances that we all do with one another whenever we are in our shadow characters. The only way to stop such a dance is to either retreat from the situation (while usually still harboring the energy of our shadow thoughts and feelings) or to choose to get into our heart and our Loving Self (see exercise in Key 8).

Now make a list of ALL of the above shadow characters that you are aware of being active within you and that you bring out onto the stage of your life from time to time (or perhaps daily). Reflect on how each of the shadow characters affects your life and your relationships. Become aware of how you feel physically whenever each character is activated. You may suddenly realize that you get headaches whenever you are in your Critical One, or stomachaches when in the Woeful One, or feel incredibly fatigued or depressed when in your Powerless One or Numb One. Make a list of each of the feelings or physical issues you become aware of when you reflect on each shadow character. This may be quite enlightening for you. If and when you feel you are ready to release any or all of those shadow characters that are active within you, proceed to the following exercise.

Why would someone not want to let go of a shadow character? We each created these characters as a form of ego defense when we were children. There was a time when we believed that each character provided some form of safety or security for us or enabled us to gain attention or positive response from others. They become habits that are as comfortable as old shoes until we become fully aware of them and the negative impact each has on our life and our relationships. They prevent us from expressing the loving true essence that we each are. We have outgrown our old childhood shoes.

2. Choosing to Release Your Cast of Shadow Characters Exercise:
Make a list of the shadow characters that you have chosen to release from the above exercise. Keep the list close at hand in case you need to peek out at it during the following meditation exercise. Find a quiet place with no distractions, noise or telephones to perform this exercise as it may take a few minutes and you will wish to be undisturbed and focus solely on what you are doing.

Get into a comfortable position either sitting or lying down. Close your eyes. Take a slow, deep breath and as you exhale feel your muscles begin to relax. Take two more slow, deep breaths, and as you exhale feel your muscles relaxing even more. Spend a moment getting into your heart by picturing someone you have a great love for, as if they were standing in front of you. Look into their eyes and feel their love and compassion flowing to you, and feel your love flowing over to them. Continue to feel this loving connection with them for a few moments until you feel warmth and an expansion or fullness in your heart. You are now in your Loving Self.

Now visualize, sense or feel yourself with all of your chosen shadow characters standing in a group in front of you; they are all facing you. Look into the eyes of each of your shadow characters as they stand before you. Look even deeper into their eyes and become aware of their sadness and confusion.

Tell each shadow character that you forgive them for being so angry, frightened, cruel, powerless, guilty, spineless, sarcastic, blind, phony, inconsiderate, worthless, isolated, complaining, resistant, non-committal, suffering, judgmental, controlling, manipulative, dutiful, numb, confused or whatever they are. Ask that they forgive you for tethering them to you for such a long time. Tell them that you don't need their assistance any longer because you now know that there is a better way. Tell them that you are ready to create more joy in your life. Ask them if they are ready to go to a place where they can experience absolute unconditional love and acceptance. Give each of your shadow characters a hug and tell them that you love them. Ask them if they are ready to go.

Now picture a column of beautiful golden-white light coming down from above, over you and the group of shadow characters. Now lift the characters either one at a time or as a group, whichever makes more sense to you, up the column of light. Lift them with your breath-- each in-breath will lift them higher and lighter, lighter and freer, faster and higher up the column of golden-white light. Follow their progress as you lift them all the way up and out the top of the column of light. Continue to lift each shadow character up the column of golden-white light until they have all disappeared. Continue to repeat the process as necessary until they are all gone.

If you are having a little difficulty with a particular shadow character, then sense yourself standing before them once again. Look deeply into their eyes once more and ask yourself what is still tethering you to this shadow self. Tell them that you forgive them and ask that they forgive you for holding on to them for so long. Tell them yet again that it is time for you to move forward in your life and make choices from a place of love rather than from fear. Give them a hug and tell them that you love them once more. Ask them if they are ready to go now; and then lift them up the column of Light when they and you are ready.

Continue the process until all the chosen shadow characters have returned to the Light. Feel the sense of peace and freedom once you have released them from your energy.

Note: You may have to complete this process in more than one session as it can be like peeling layers of an onion at times. Sometimes we find that we are not quite ready to release a specific energy from our field so immediately. Be aware of how this energy is affecting you negatively so that you can make a loving choice to release it. If this is difficult, try to understand what is tethering you to this particular shadow self and whether or not it would be beneficial to keep yourself tethered to it. Do not judge yourself. Only you know when you are ready to release each of these energies. Everything happens in its own time.

It is not unusual for us to recreate some shadow characters on occasion as they have been with us for so long and seem so familiar (like a HABIT), especially during times where we feel stressed, vulnerable, unloved, angry, lonely or disconnected. It is important to attempt to understand what triggers you to go into this shadow self. Once you acknowledge what the situations are that trigger you, you can empower yourself to make a more informed choice to either create from your shadows or from your loving self.

3. Preparation for Garden of Creation Exercise: Make a list of your five most heartfelt desires that you wish to create in your life. These should be goals, wishes or energies that will bring you great joy, peace and happiness once they are manifested. Examples may include physical health, more love in your life or your home, finding a life partner, improved tennis game, financial abundance, more harmonious relationships, joy, connectedness, specific goals in business, pursuit of one's life passion or purpose, being the next winner of American Idol, etc.

There are no limits to what you can choose to create. You are limited only by the limits you place on your self, your imagination, your fear of failure or the box you choose to stand within. Now is the time to step out of the box you have created for yourself and create your self or your life anew. On a piece of paper draw a symbol to represent each of your five most heartfelt desires that you are choosing to manifest. This is an important step so that when you do the following creation meditation exercise you will be able to picture or visualize what that goal or desire actually "looks like".

4. Garden of Creation Meditation:

Hint- This meditation will be more effective if you have a friend read it with feeling to you or you record yourself reading it with heart on an audio tape and play it back to follow as you meditate in a quiet private space. This meditation can also be found on a companion CD that accompanies this book (for details see www.12keystoshift.com *).*

Close your eyes. Take a slow, deep, relaxing breath and as you exhale feel all of your tension releasing from your body. Take two more slow, deep, relaxing breaths and as you exhale feel your muscles relaxing even more. Now see, sense or feel yourself standing in the most beautiful garden that you have ever seen. The sights, sounds and scents of this incredible garden fill every cell of your being. You notice a path leading you deeper into the garden. Follow the path and it will lead you to a small building emanating bright white light.

Place your hand on the door and feel the incredible energy emanating from this small building. This is your creative space within your Garden of Creation. When you open the door and enter your creative space, you will find a room filled with intense white light. You will use this light to begin to manifest whatever is your most heartfelt desire to create in your life. Now enter the room.

Begin to create your heartfelt desires as if they already exist at this moment. See each detail of your creation. See yourself interacting with your creation with your family, friends, loved ones, and the world. Work quickly from your heart without getting into your mind too much about what you are creating. Create from your loving self rather than from your mind. Send your creation love from your heart as you create. When you have finished one goal, move to the next.

Once you are finished with your creations, send your love to all that you have created and step back out of your creative space into the beautiful garden. When you feel that you are ready to return to your physical world, gently open your eyes.

During the course of your day, send your love intermittently to your creations that are in your creative space in your Garden of Creation. There is no limit to what you can create in your garden of creation. You may return to your Garden of Creation at any time.

5. Energy Medicine Techniques:
Hydrate and do the 3 thumps before proceeding.

1.This exercise will help you lift your unwanted shadow characters which you may have trouble releasing or let you be more forgiving of yourself if you don't want to let them go. On a scale from 0 (none) to 10 (most) evaluate the level of distress the following statements provoke before your tapping session so that you can note improvements.

2.Treat the possibility of reversal by repeating one (or any that strongly resonate with you) of the following phrases three times with feeling while tapping on the KC point (if you want to be more specific for your situation, then by all means modify them; phrases you don't use now you can use in subsequent rounds):

"Even though I feel so (fill in the blank… angry, powerless, defiant, resentful, fearful, cynical, controlling, judgmental, abusive), and I don't know how to let this feeling go, I deeply and completely love and accept myself with all of my feelings."

"Even though I am so confused in my thinking and know that I create chaos in my life for… whatever reason (fill in the whatever reason and be as specific as you can), I completely love and accept myself anyway with all my feelings and ask the universe for assistance in helping me to create from my heart."

"Even though I am too afraid to change my perception of being a victim and blaming others for my problems and choices, I now choose to completely love and accept myself anyway, even if I find that changing my thoughts is difficult."

"Even though I don't feel safe in the world if I don't try to please others and/or protect myself by being: The Furious One, The Scared One, The Cruel One, The Powerless One, The Guilty One, The Pleasing Caretaker, The Sarcastic One, The Sightless One, The Fake One, The Inconsiderate One, The Worthless One, The Secluded One, The Defiant One, The Dissatisfied One, The Evasive One, The Woeful One, The Critical One, The Scheming One, The Obedient One, The Frozen (Numb/Empty) One, and The Confused One, I completely love and accept myself and choose to transform this shadow thought now."

"Even though I am afraid if I change and let go of (any of the above shadow characters), others will be confused, won't know what to do and it will likely change our relationship, I choose to completely love and accept myself anyway with all of my feelings."

"Even though I feel helpless to change, don't know what the consequences will be and have no control anyway, I deeply love and accept myself with all my feelings."

"Even though I don't want to let go of (insert name of shadow character) and know I am not capable of changing anyway, I deeply and completely love, forgive and accept myself anyway with all my feelings."

3. Then tap on the following points seven times while thinking about whichever statements above gave you the biggest buzz or level of distress: EB, SE, UE, UN, Ch, CB, UA, and TH.

4. Once again rate your feeling on a 0 to 10 scale. If there is no significant decrease in the rating, go back to step 2 and do 3 more rounds of tapping with feeling. Be sure you are emotionally tuned in to the problem. You may utilize the 9 Gamut Procedure/ sandwich technique if you continue to have difficulty diminishing the feeling of guilt or shame.

5. In the event you still have no results, look for another phrase, which resonates more for you, reword step two with the new phrase and do 3 more rounds of tapping.

6. As long as your level of distress continues to decrease, keep tapping until there is little or none left. If the treatment still stalls, try tapping on your KC point and say three times with feeling: "Even though I still have some of these feelings or beliefs, I deeply and completely love and accept myself" and do some more rounds of tapping. Repeat as necessary.

7. You may choose to do the 9 gamut or the short cut procedure as described below if you still have problems reducing your guilt, shame, unworthiness or sense of disconnection from God/Source/Spirit level down to a 1 or a 0.

In the 9 Gamut Procedure, you must first locate the gamut point on the back of either hand, 1/2 inch beyond the knuckles (toward the wrist), and in line with the midpoint between the pinky finger and the ring finger. While constantly tapping the gamut point, do the following nine actions:

1. Close eyes.
2. Open eyes.
3. While holding the head still, shift eyes to lower left.
4. While holding head still, move eyes to lower right.
5. Roll eyes clockwise 360 degrees while keeping head still.
6. Roll eyes counter-clockwise 360 degrees while holding head still.
7. Hum a few bars of your favorite tune for a few seconds (e.g., "Somewhere Over the Rainbow", "Happy Birthday," "Row, Row Your Boat.")
8. Count to five.
9. Hum once again.

OR try the short version by tapping on your gamut spot while holding your head straight and moving only your eyes down to the floor and then up toward the ceiling.

As you repeat these treatments over time, the negative feeling or shadow thought should go away.

6. Daily Intention Exercise:

Every morning before you get out of bed (or during the quietest moment of your day) set your intention for what you choose to create in your day. What do you have the greatest desire to draw to you today? It may be a dream you have held onto for years, it may be drawing more love into a relationship, or a new job or career path.... You are only limited by your imagination. Take a quick trip to your creative space in your Garden of Creation and see this creation as if it has already happened and walk into your day as if it is on its way to you.

7. Every 6 Months Intention Exercise:

Every six months, take the time to create a poster that sets your intentions for the next 6 months. Have fun with this. This can be a great exercise to do with a partner or with a small group of friends.

Get a few old magazines (ones you do not mind cutting up). It doesn't matter what kind of magazines as long as they have pictures in them. Put on some relaxing music and pass around the magazines. Stay in your heart rather than in your head while you do this exercise.

As you look through the magazines, tear out any pages that have a picture or words that resonate for you as being something that you have a sincere desire to create or draw to you in your life. Once you have gone through all of the magazines and have a pile of pages in front of you, use scissors to cut out the pictures and/or words that you have collected.

Next, arrange the cut out collection of pictures and words that you have acquired in whatever way you wish onto a piece of poster board or onto a piece of cardboard. Glue the pieces into place.

Once everyone has finished their intention poster, have everyone take turns sharing what is on their posters and what it represents to them. It can be very powerful to express your intentions out loud in the vibration of your own voice.

Now place the poster somewhere in your home where you will see it every day. Spend a moment every day reviewing your intention poster and sending your sincere heartfelt desire toward your creations on your poster daily. At the end of 6 months, notice how many of your intentions manifested in your life.

Applying Key 11:

Example 1. Andrea is a 44-year-old single female who originally presented for treatment of post-traumatic stress disorder and severe recurrent depression. I had first treated her when I was in my second year of residency training after medical school. I treated her with medication and insight-oriented psychotherapy for 4 years but could no longer treat her when I took a position at a state psychiatric hospital facility where they did not allow any outpatient treatment of patients. At the time of termination of her therapy, she asked if she could return as a patient in the future if I ever went into private practice and she found out where I was practicing. I told her that I would certainly be willing to work with her again if she continued to have a desire to change. She had been abstinent from substances for about a year at the time of completion of my initial treatment of her but she continued to suffer from depression and anxiety and continued to create chaotic relationships. I wished her well and transferred her care to another treating psychiatrist just prior to my relocation for my new position.

I returned to the area a few years later and set up a private psychiatric practice. I was somewhat surprised to receive a call one day from Andrea whom I had not heard from since her termination of treatment 4 years prior. The following is her story in her own words:

"This is part of my journey that I feel necessary to write down. Not only to remind me of where I've been but the progress I've made. I was strung out on heroin and various other drugs, when I called Dr. Tracy Latz's office to see if I could see her. I was crying and the secretary interrupted her session to see. Dr. Latz offered to see me. She did so, knowing that I was on disability and couldn't pay for it. She saw me pro-bono. When I first went to see her, I thought I looked good. Five foot six inches; I was dressed up weighing 110 pounds max. She was straightforward with me and told me I looked 'like hell'. That threw me off. She continued to see me. My life was in total turmoil. She gave me hope, which I hadn't had in a long time. Once I got clean, she started showing me a new way of life. On route to a spiritual way of life, I struggled because I didn't believe in religion. But she stayed with me. My appreciation and gratitude are more than words can grasp. Sometimes I just cry because I'm so thankful. Without using the words religion and/or God she showed me the way to my inner sanctuary. As I learned to apply her teachings in my daily life, I continued to learn and grow. In spite of my struggles with God and religion I learned that spiritual doesn't mean the same. I learned how to live and make choices that were healthy for me. Never, in my life, did I make healthy choices. In and out of bad relationships plus the numerous abuses I suffered in my early childhood and as an adult. My 'doc', otherwise known as Dr. Tracy Latz, stood by me and taught me this new way of life. As long as I practiced the principles and made good choices my life would continue to change. And it has. It's absolutely amazing to me the changes that have come about. Far from 'perfect', but incredible just the same. I'm 44 and been drinking since I was 9 and started doing drugs by 14. There's not many drugs that I haven't done. I'm not sure how long it took because I had to get free from the drugs and get a clear head. I did struggle many days, to get out of a chaotic life. Once I did the changes began to happen. My doc could have given up on me many times, but she didn't. I hope many, many people can grasp this and change their lives. It's wonderful and amazing. All thanks to 'my doc'."

It is of note that when Andrea first came to my new office, she was malnourished, in a physically and emotionally abusive relationship, addicted to drugs, and living out of her car that was no longer in working condition. As she began to understand who she really was and began to shift, she became clean and sober, chose healthier relationships with less chaos, and moved into a safe, clean apartment of her own. She began to have more regard for her own personal safety and more compassion overall for herself.

Andrea is a wonderful example of how we all can learn when the desire is deep enough. We can all choose to reinvent ourselves and recreate our lives. However, we must first decide what we no longer desire or what no longer "grows corn" for us. Then we must decide what we want to draw to us in our life. Andrea is a perfect example of someone who actively chooses every day to create more positive experiences and relationships. The next example will show how we can also very powerfully choose to create from our shadows.

Example 2: Lincoln is a 35-year-old divorced female who originally came to my office for treatment of severe depression following a fetal demise at 7 months into her pregnancy. She responded partially to antidepressant medication; however, she improved much more dramatically when she began to understand her own power to create in her life and actively used the tools conveyed in this book. She began to consciously create positive experiences and less drama and chaos in her life. She felt she was making wonderful progress as she made new friends and was active in community activities. She eventually moved away to another state.

I heard back from her approximately a year later. She started off her session with, "I KNOW that this makes me a bad person – BUT!" She then described how she had "stopped using my tools" (i.e., she began to sleepwalk in life again), and she had become involved with a man who was already in a relationship with another woman. She had known all along that he was committed to this other person but decided to pursue the relationship anyway. She reported that her lover had informed her that this other woman was now pregnant with their second child. He told Lincoln that their relationship was over, as he felt more committed to the mother of his children.

Lincoln was extremely distraught, disappointed, angry, desperate, and felt terribly abandoned. She then contacted her now ex-lover a few days later to inform him that she was also pregnant... knowing full well that this was a lie and a ruse to lure him back into her life. She told me in her session that she knew this was not the morally right thing to do; from her 12 Key teachings, she knew she could not be creating anything positive in her life. However, she stated she intended to follow this through to see if he would leave the mother of his children to be with her. She actually told me that she was going to go to her Garden of Creation and create this man leaving the mother of his children and deciding to be with her. I cautioned her strongly; reminding her that she can only create for herself and NOT for anyone else. She stated she knew this, but that she again was going ahead with her plan anyway.

At this point she was making a conscious choice to create chaos in her life with her anger, resentment, and fear as she desired to control another person's divine will. We discussed this choice openly in her session and the potential consequences of what she would be attracting. She replied, "I know…. But I want this." In that moment she felt happy with her decision. When I heard back from her the following week, she was once again very distraught and at the same time excited. She reported that she had missed her own menstrual period and had checked a home pregnancy test and that IT WAS POSITIVE! She was beginning to get attention from her male suitor again who was beginning to feel torn between his responsibilities. However, her former lover had informed her that he was still not going to leave his other relationship. She angrily stated that she intended to follow through with this presumed pregnancy just to punish this man; not out of love for the child she believed she was carrying, but out of a sense of revenge.

Once again we discussed at length the power of her intention. She was very much aware that she was looking at potentially giving birth to and raising a child, out of resentment and rage over not being the chosen partner of her lover. We discussed the potential hardships that both she and this child might face in light of her choice. She was not willing to listen to or entertain a different creation in her life. Interestingly enough, when she went to a physician to have the progress of the pregnancy confirmed, she was informed that she had what was known as a molar pregnancy. This is a term used to describe a FALSE pregnancy where the BODY is CONVINCED that there is a viable fetus; however, there is only placental tissue present in the uterus. It is a fairly rare occurrence and must be terminated, as it will continue to grow extremely rapidly, like a cancer. When her family and male suitor found out about this, they couldn't understand the condition and everyone just called her a liar.

Her thoughts and powerful intention created a situation in perfect harmony. The power of her lie, in what she thought and spoke in conjunction with her intense desire to make it so, created very powerfully and rapidly the physical manifestation of the same lie in her own body. The joke was on her.... a joke of her own creation. She was not a victim of anyone or anything except for her own self. I do not judge her in any fashion. There is something for each of us to learn very powerfully whether we create from our shadows or create from our heart. Sometimes we need to learn who we are NOT before we are ready to truly understand who we are.

I honor Lincoln and her use of her own divine free will in her journey. It is equally important to understand that the man in this scenario was rapidly creating his own experiences just as powerfully for he had attracted Lincoln into his life as well. There was something essential for both of them to learn from this situation.

Example 3: I have a 7-year-old niece (one of a set of twin girls) who was born with a severe heart defect. She had emergency heart surgery at 2 days of age to create an artery to one of her lungs and to surgically repair a hole in her heart and create another artery connection coming out of her heart. She had her second surgery at 4 years old when she was old enough to be aware of the doctors and needles and the pain when she was exhibiting signs of congestive heart failure.

She is now old enough that she has finally begun to question why she has had heart surgeries and neither of her 2 siblings and especially her twin sister has not. She is beginning to ask if the "pinchy doctors" are going to have to work on her heart again. She wants to know if she will have her chest opened again and her heart opened again. She is very curious but also beginning to express increasing fear over the possibility of another surgery. She will have to have another surgery when she turns around 12 or 13 years of age as her created arteries will be too small to support the needed increase in blood flow as she grows. There was some concern that she might even require a sooner surgery since her new artery created to go to her lung has over the past few years developed a kink as it was not growing in proportion to the rest of her body. She does not know this, as her parents are concerned about creating too much anticipatory fear of what is not likely to happen for several years.

Ever since Sydney could practically talk, she was all but obsessed with Peter Pan while her twin sister was as obsessed with Tinker Bell.

Sydney would only want green clothes (like Peter Pan) and she would repetitively sing the song "I don't want to grow up" that she had learned from watching the animated Peter Pan Disney movie over and over. It struck me before her second heart surgery that perhaps it wouldn't be such a great thing for her to fill her mind and thoughts with the idea of never growing up. I spoke with my brother and asked if I might present her with a gift that I felt might somehow help her. He was open to the idea.

So the week before Sydney's heart surgery at 4 years of age I presented her with a beautiful crystal (amethyst and quartz) wand and talked with her about picturing herself dancing in a rainbow and using her magic wand to heal her heart (this was at a time when she could barely move across the room quickly without panting and having to lay down). We created the association of the song "Somewhere Over the Rainbow" with the image of her dancing in a rainbow freely without any effort or tiredness... she really responded well to this image and would giggle and smile each time she did the visualization. I gave her a cd with 12 different versions of the song on it (from Judy Garland to country to rock and roll to jazz) and she listened to it every night as she was going to sleep the week before her surgery. It would play through the night over and over as she slept in the room with her twin sister.

I was with Sydney and her parents in the holding room before her surgery at 4 years old as we all quietly sang "Somewhere Over the Rainbow" to her as she was holding her wand in one hand and began to go under with iv anesthesia. She did this smiling without any anxiety or worry although the rest of us were in tears shortly after she was unconscious. We had cartoons on in the pediatric holding room and as she drifted off to sleep there was suddenly a Magic School Bus cartoon that came on the screen that showed the cartoon characters all dancing in the sky in a rainbow. My eyes opened wide and locked onto my brother's eyes that were exact mirrors of mine. Could it be a coincidence?

She still really likes the song but has no real memory of the reason why it is so prominent for her. I saw her around the fourth of July of 2007 and spoke with her about her fears. I told her to close her eyes and just picture herself dancing in a rainbow of light and holding the wand (that she still keeps in her bedroom) while the song "Somewhere

Over the Rainbow" is playing. She smiled and opened her eyes and said "Aunt Tracy, that really makes me happy."

I got a call from my brother at the end of August 2007 and he was thrilled to inform me that Sydney had been given great news at her follow-up cardiologist appointment. It appears that her artery to her lung has somehow miraculously corrected itself. Of course, the real test of this approach will be at the time of her next heart surgery, whenever that is to occur, in the future. For now, it seemed to help alleviate her bubbling angst as she questions why she is different from everyone else and what that potentially means for her future.... And perhaps it had something to do with her artery suddenly growing and straightening itself out after three years.

KEY 12: The Obstacle of Self-Discipline: Stay Connected Every Day

How do we remain conscious and centered creating from our heart and not our negative thoughts or feelings in this crazy fast paced world we live in? If you have diligently progressed through all of the previous 11 Keys presented in this book, you will have removed all the potential obstacles or roadblocks that you have unwittingly placed in your way and you are now capable of experiencing joy and peace on a daily basis in your life. Since we are "human beings" and our existence does not cease from this current enlightened moment in our life, we are unfortunately at daily risk, if we are not mindful, of recreating our blocks -- our stuckness.

To survive the daily stress, negative emotions and thoughts that we encounter daily we need to have a regular routine that keeps us balanced in body, mind and spirit. Various cultures and religions approach this dilemma in many different ways using a daily centering practice called Dharma. This term refers to a form of self-discipline ranging from prayer to yoga to whatever regular practice assists you with feeling balanced and connected to the whole. In all cultures, the importance of a meditative practice is emphasized, whether that be a prayerful meditation, a walking meditation, tai chi, breath work, drumming, toning or chanting sacred mantras, self healing (Reiki) or meaningful body movement which is both connecting and grounding.

In earlier Keys we have given you techniques that may also serve as Daily Dharma if they resonate for you. These include acknowledging your blessings, breathing exercises, mindfulness meditations, toning, tapping affirmations or utilizing the various meditations we have presented to you.

Create Your Own Daily Dharma:
1. Create a Place of Tranquility:
Create your own sacred space, which may be a place in your home or a place where you go to be in tranquility or prayerful meditation on a regular basis. This can be an area of a room or something as specific as an altar that you make spiritual or important to yourself through intention. You can adorn it with candles, incense burners, bells, beads, photos, or anything with personal meaning, religious or otherwise. Perform your daily routine in this special space. The size of this space may be as small as a windowsill or as large as your backyard. Whatever space you have available and resonates with you should work just fine.

2. The Awareness Garden Journaling Exercise:
Begin to keep a daily awareness journal in which you document the quality of your daily thoughts and feelings. This journal is different from a typical journal in that you assign certain thoughts and feelings specific colors. At the end of each day, you draw a picture in your journal of a garden that represents your thoughts and feelings that you entertained on that given day.

The idea behind creating an awareness journal by color-coding your thoughts and feelings is to stay VERY AWARE of how you create your life daily. It can be likened to having a compass which will enable you to correct your course immediately and stay on track with your true self to manifest your life from your heart and not your fears and negative reactive voice.

Guide for the Ultimate Gardener
First, make a list of the positive thoughts and feelings you have and assign a color to each. Here are just a few possible examples:
Self Love = coral
Unconditional love = pink
Joy = orange

Intuitive = violet
Feeling forgiving = white
Peaceful = indigo
Hopeful = green
Abundant thinking = yellow
Expressive, introspective, calm, in harmony = blue
Spiritual = gold
Compassion = magenta

On the negative side, determine which colors resonate with your feelings of: sadness, depression, doubt, overwhelm, confusion, hurt, abandonment, anger and resentment, inadequacy, guilt and shame, to mention a few.

Expand both of your positive and negative thoughts/emotions lists and assign the appropriate colors that resonate with you.

When you notice that your garden in your journal is looking less than beautiful, then you know that it is time to go to the garden shed, take out your tools and put them into practice. You have learned throughout the 12 Keys that to maintain the garden of your thoughts and feelings in all its optimal beauty requires: weeding, fertilizing or watering EVERY DAY. Use the tool most likely to assist you in either transforming any negative thoughts or feelings into positive ones, or to enhance the good thoughts and feelings.

Note how stuck it feels to have those correspondingly negative colors in your garden. Feel how wonderful and vibrant it feels to have all those lovely colors corresponding to love, joy and abundance. Decide daily how you are going to continue to create. Remember that we are on a journey of self-discovery and to shift and change requires acknowledgement, awareness and practice. Journal daily and acknowledge your progress.

3. Color Focus Exercise:
This exercise allows you to get in touch with your sense of connection, inner strength and wisdom daily.

Close your eyes and take a few slow, deep breaths. Imagine a beautiful indigo sky filled with brilliant stars and planets. Sense the peace you feel knowing that you are never alone. Feel your deep connection and sense of inner wisdom in knowing that you are directly linked to all the knowledge and power of the universe.

Focus on the indigo color in the night sky. Breathe it into every atom, cell and molecule of your body. Now, see, sense or feel the color indigo filling your body with all the strength and support of all the positive and wonderful energy in the universe. Feel the color indigo filling you with this sense of strength and peace. Stay with this feeling and open your eyes when you are ready.

4. Time Out For Mindfulness:

If you have never done this before, you don't know what you are missing. This exercise is to remind you to enjoy the power of now, live in the present and acknowledge that each day is a journey unto itself. The best part about it is you don't have to DO anything. This seems simple, but it is not easy.

Every day take a block of time, whether it's 15 minutes or an hour; whatever you need or desire. Cut out all the chatter in your head, stop multi–tasking, FOCUS and be present for whatever you are doing-- or not. You can just BE during this time. Do nothing, meditate, or take a walk while being aware of the sounds and sensations surrounding you. Perhaps it is just listening to the crunch of the leaves or snow underfoot, feeling the warmth of the rays of the sun on your body, hearing the wind rustling through the leaves, etc. You get the picture; it's about experiencing the moment. In fact you can do anything you are involved in, as long as you are focused on the present moment and are feeling that moment with all its sensations without distraction.

If you are undisciplined and habitually multi-task, you will likely need to remove all potential distractions before you begin to attempt this exercise. Turn off your phones, televisions, computers or other sources of predictable distraction; announce to the world that you need some time for yourself and go for it.

5. Reiki Prayer:

We are both Reiki masters and teach this prayer to our students on a regular basis. It is a simple, yet very powerful, tool and we both say it each morning upon rising:

For today only anger not, worry not.
Be grateful and humble.
Do your work with appreciation.
Be kind to all.

This prayer essentially reminds us to be detached from anything that we essentially have no control over (such as any other person's thoughts, feelings or actions) and how we believe things or conditions need to be or should be. It helps us to reduce the expectations that cause disappointment. It also reminds us to be fully present in the moment, neither worrying about the past nor the future. After all, we are very powerful in our choices; and we can only choose in the present since the past has already happened and the future has not yet occurred. If we are not fully in the present, we will miss all of our opportunities to choose and create mindfully. This prayer also reinforces the awareness that we should be mindful of being kind to all and not fall back into living in our egos. We live daily with gratitude in our hearts and awareness that we are no more and no less than anyone else.

Applying Key 12:

Example 1: Hanna is a 38-year-old married female with three active children. She presented with complaints of obsessive thoughts and endless chatter in her head. Her anxiety stemmed from feeling helpless and powerless to effectively control every aspect of everyone's life in her family. She felt it was her duty to make everything perfect and to fix any situation that was not, in her mind, as it "should be". She was in a constant state of stress, manifesting in frequent headaches and sleepless nights.

Hanna reported that, despite her enmeshment in the lives of her family, she had never been present for either her husband or her children since the chatter in her head never gave her the peace of mind to listen. She also wondered whether anyone ever heard what she had to say, as she had felt invisible and unheard as a child. Hanna's father was an alcoholic and described as verbally abusive, irrational when drunk, uncaring and unreliable. When Hanna was a young teenager, her father had frequently thrown heavy objects at her mother, barely missing Hanna and her siblings on several occasions.

As an adult, Hanna was anxious about everything that could possibly happen in the future. The world was not a safe place. Her fear was related to the belief that danger could be lurking anywhere around the next corner; everything was out of her direct control. Anything could happen at any time! When was the next shoe going to drop – or the vase fly across the room? Hanna had little trust in her own judgment and no trust in the judgment of others. She was very unforgiving of both herself and others for not being perfect.

Hanna had difficulty getting out of her head, so she initially best benefited from the tapping techniques in each of the 12 Keys. Hanna began to tap regularly for not needing to be perfect in various situations. Then she began tapping protocols for forgiving herself for her inability to forgive herself and others. Soon thereafter, she began regularly tapping in affirmations that she was perfect just the way she was. From that point on, she tapped several times a day to reduce her anxiety and obsessive thoughts.

After a few weeks, she was finally ready to do the meditations in the various Keys to transform her negative thoughts and emotions; and the journaling exercise described above became her chief daily Dharma. This exercise created awareness for Hanna of the quality of thoughts she was thinking on a daily basis. She had never been so aware of where she focused her attention before. This Dharma helped her to choose to focus differently and shift.

Hanna has cut out most of her chatter in her head now and likes feeling present in the moment, which she had never truly experienced before. She reports, " I never knew how good I could feel, because I had never experienced the feeling of being centered and calm without all the chatter". Her headaches are gone and she is peacefully sleeping through the night.

Example 2: Charlotte is a 55-year-old single female who has struggled with depression and weight issues for most of her life. She came to the 12 Keys "searching for something to make my life more complete". She has utilized all of the techniques we teach over the past three years. She has developed her own routine or daily Dharma to keep herself present in the moment that includes swimming, meditation, mindfulness and she particularly likes the above awareness garden journaling exercise:

"The 12 Keys proved you can find inner peace, clarity, productivity just by creating your own inner space and setting your intention. These techniques developed my meditation and visualization abilities by practicing daily, and I was never aware before that I possessed those abilities. They are now healing to me every day. You see, I am the gardener, the creator of my life experiences. I now see a lot of flowers that bring me back to my true essence. I recall a poem I read years ago-

> Your mind is a garden
> Your thoughts are the seeds
> The harvest can be either flower or weeds

Well, the weeds represent the past, anything that blocked my Spirit from shining. As the gardener of my garden I can grant myself a clean slate. The love I am seeking is the Love I am."

Example 3: Mark is a 39-year-old married male who had felt an inner restlessness and a sense that there must be more to life than his, in his eyes, mundane existence. However, he now feels his life has more meaning and passion; and he feels a greater sense of connectedness. He has become very disciplined in making certain that he remains connected by using what he has learned through the 12 Keys teachings every day. In his own words:

"The 12 Keys has been a blessing; that's the best term I can use today. It is life altering, yet so familiar. It is like coming home. It's been there all along, but I had forgotten it, lost sight of it, or rejected it in favor of logic. It is a place of peacefulness, exhilaration, direction and truthful insight. Thank you for making this teaching available!"

"Descartes said, 'I think therefore I am'. What is wrong with 'I am therefore I am?' Too god-like? We impose a separation from the divine. But if our incarnation is of a divine source, why are we less than divine? Our language seems to not permit adequate description of our relationship to that which is divine. Language is left-brain driven; the meditations given within the 12 Keys are the sanctuary of the right brain. It defies linguistic description. Ironically, it is the experience, the empiricism, of the 12 Key teachings that is its best witness. You just have to do it to understand it. The teachings do not conflict with any contemporary religion. If the 12 Keys are jolting at all, it is in its ability to make sense of the Christian (or any other religion's) message; it is 'the best of the best' so to speak, shedding the politics of religion in favor of the original messages that are mythological – meaning transcending of particular cultures, and true to humanity."

"The training is so informative that it can take time to integrate it all. I would like to find a vehicle in which to share these teachings with others and support those who are making the trainings possible. This needs to be shared with as many people as possible!"

Beyond the Keys: Life After Stepping Into the Powerful Creative Being That You Are

So, where do you go from here? That is essentially up to you. Your vision of your purpose and how you choose to see yourself within the bigger picture is essential in terms of shifting your consciousness. To get unstuck and shift means to change your perceptions about yourself and the way you view your world.

We hope that you have found the tools in the 12 Keys that resonate for you and will assist you with achieving your goals. Everyone will have a different journey for we each have our own unique physical and emotional experiences. Some might feel a profound calling from their spirit or True Essence to be of service to others or to follow their own specific path.

Your progress won't necessarily be linear. We guarantee that regular tests and challenges will arise enabling you to make different choices, raise your consciousness, shift and grow. Understand that you are never finished with your journey. So many people are looking for that guru or teacher who is going to hand them the golden apple that will allow them to suddenly be fully balanced, present and healed for the rest of their life. Then their work will be done. There is no such guru, as the real teacher is within us all. You are never done.

You always have the capacity to grow emotionally or spiritually. When you stop growing and begin to sleepwalk through your experiences, you will likely become stuck again. If you do, then pick up the 12 Keys and use it to shift whatever is creating you stuck once again. When you feel stuck, the teacher within is trying to capture your attention. You must be aware, open to listen and make the choice to shift.

We wish you well in your journey as you blossom more fully at deeper levels in your life.

Tracy & Marion

Appendix

A. Self care protocols:
1. Correction for Excess Energy Technique:

Our imbalance in the meridians can come from being over-charged and having too much energy. This results in feeling spaced out, confused or overwhelmed. To correct for over-energy: Cross the left ankle over the right, extend arms with backs of hands facing each other, bring right hand over left, clasp fingers together, fold arms and hands inward and rest on the chest under the chin; rest tongue on the roof of your mouth behind your front teeth, breathe deeply for 1-2 minutes. It's very calming for most individuals and can be used as a separate exercise to promote sleep and reduce acute anxiety.

2. The Three Thumps:

This routine comes from the ancient Chinese method of balancing the energy flow of the body by tapping certain points on acupuncture meridians.

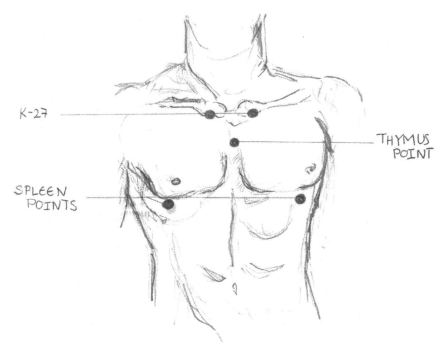

Tap each point for 30 seconds

Tap the K-27 points under the collarbone near the sternum or breastbone. This is the top point of the kidney meridian. This is a great point for keeping your energies moving forward, energizing your body and improving focus.

Tap the thymus point in the sternum to stimulate the immune system and boost your vitality. This point is found in the following manner: Lightly place your index fingertip at the top of your breastbone (below the Adam's apple). Now slowly trace your fingertip downwards approximately 2 to 2 1/2 inches and you will notice that there is a slight bony bulge. You are now at the level of the thymus.

Tap the spleen point under your breasts to energize and balance the body's energy system. In men this point may be found approximately 3 inches below the nipple. In women this point may be found mid-nipple line, approximately one thumb's width below where the wire of an underwire bra would lay against the body.

3. Zipping Up Your Central Meridian:

This essential daily exercise assists you to feel strong, centered and protects your good energies from negative energy coming in from the outside. The electromagnetic energy flowing from your hand moves the energy in the meridian.

Place either hand on or just a few inches in front of your pubic bone over the center of your body (the beginning of your central meridian). With intention, breathe in slowly and deeply as you move your hand up the center of your body to the level of the bottom of your lower lip. Repeat this maneuver with your hand three times and after the third sweep imagine that you have a key to lock in all of your good energy while keeping out negative influences from the energy of others and the environment. This is a good technique to protect yourself from all those energy vampires out there who can drain you energetically. It also is a good technique for people who are very empathic and overly sensitive to picking up anxiety or negative vibes from others. You may do this as often as needed throughout the day.

4. Tapping Points

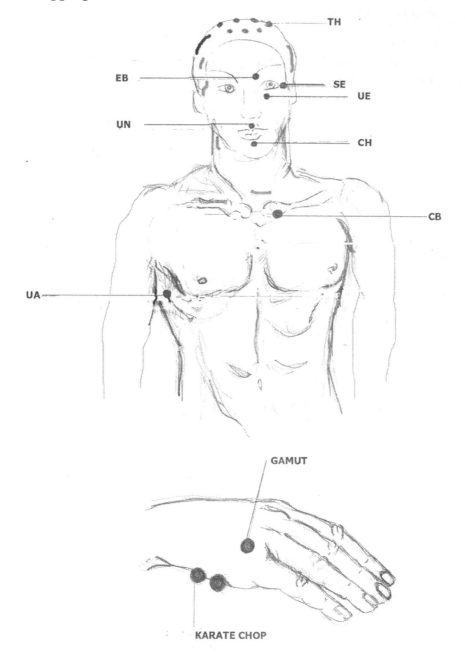

Bibliography

Eden, Donna, Feinstein David, *Energy Medicine*, New York: Jeremy Tarcher/Putnam, 1998.

Feinstein, David, Eden, Donna, Craig Gary, *The Promise of Energy Psychology*, New York, Tarcher/Penguin, 2005.

Gallo, Fred, *Energy Diagnostic and Treatment Methods*, New York, W.W. Norton, 2000.

Gerber, Richard, M.D.   *A Practical Guide To Vibrational Medicine*, New York, Harper and Collins Publishers, 2000.

Germer, Christopher, Siegel, Ronald, Fulton, Paul, *Mindfulness and Psychotherapy*, New York, Guilford Press, 2005.

Judith, Anodea, *Wheels Of Life*, St. Paul, Llwellyn Publications, 2000.

Phillips, Maggie, *Finding the Energy to Heal: How EMDR, Hypnosis, TFT Imagery and Body - Focused Therapy Can Help Resolve Health Problems*, New York, W.W.Norton, 2000.

Index

Printed in the United States
134940LV00001B/284/P